VISUAL GUIDE THE EXPIATORY TEMPLE OF

La Sagrada Familia

PHOTOGRAPHS: CARLOS GIORDANO AND NICOLÁS PALMISANO

GUÍAS VISUALES
GRANDES OBRAS

01

02

06

07

contents

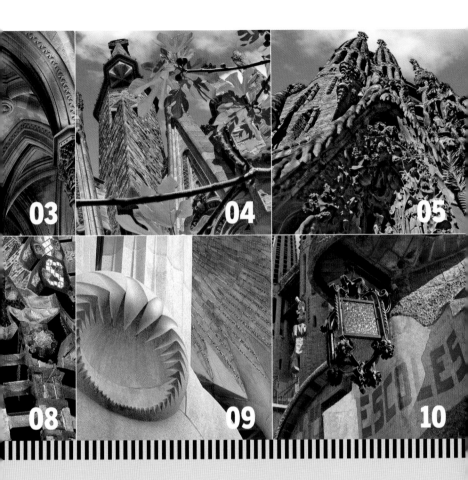

01

The origins of the temple

A glance at the events of its time

At the end of the 19th century Barcelona was a city in full industrialisation and enjoyed a rich cultural life. Its bourgeoisie promoted artistic projects of all kind, while religious spirit was gathering momentum. Within this context the temple of the Sagrada Familia was born: what started as the dream of Barcelonan, Josep Maria Bocabella, would in time become Gaudí's dream and the city's symbol.

The temple's promoter

The idea of erecting a temple in honour of the Holy Family came from Josep Maria Bocabella, a Barcelona bookseller. A learned man of strong religious conviction, Bocabella was president of the Association of Devotees to Saint Joseph.
In 1872, he travelled to Rome to offer to the Pope, in the name of the association, a silver reproduction of a picture of Sagrada Familia. Before returning to Spain he passed through the Italian village of Loreto which is famous for its basilica and where, according to tradition, is the house where Joseph, Mary and Jesus lived. Bocabella was amazed by this church and decided to make a replica in Barcelona. However, he soon abandoned the idea and opted to build a new and original temple.

Barcelona's coat of arms
The city's emblem was frequently used in the architecture of the period.

The promoter
Driven by his devotion to Saint Joseph, José Maria Bocabella wanted to dedicate a temple to the Holy Family.

The spirit of the period

In the 19th century Catalonia experienced an unprecedented cultural renewal, reflected in a spectacular rise in literary and artistic production and above all, architecture. This movement was called the *Renaixença* (Renaissance), owing to the fact that it experienced an authentic reemergence of cultural values, at a time when the Catalan language was trying to be recuperated as the official language.

CHRONOLOGY
KEY FACTS ABOUT GAUDÍ'S PERIOD

1853
Otis invents the lift
The inventor Elisha G. Otis presented the first lift with anti-fall mechanism.

1865
Abolition of slavery in the USA. The end of the American Civil War meant freedom for the slaves.

1867
The first volume of the book *The Capital*. It was in this essay that Karl Marx dissected the capitalist system.

Das Kapital.
Kritik der politischen Oekonomie
Karl Marx.

1870
The Third French Republic. King Louis Napoleon III abdicated after the defeat of France in the war against Prussia.

The house in Loreto
The basilica in Loreto was where Bocabella took the decision to build a temple in Barcelona. Within its interior is the house where apparently Jesus, Mary and Joseph lived in Nazareth.

El Propagador
Was the Association of Devotees to Saint Joseph's magazine. It was in 1873 that the idea to build a temple was published for the first time.

Bourgeoisie Splendour
Catalonia, with the city of Barcelona at its helm, was the region in Spain which most quickly adapted to the changes provoked by the Industrial Revolution. While the rest of Spain continued being basically agricultural, a solid industrial framework was being created in Catalonia. This economic prosperity led to a flourishing bourgeoisie, who became promoter, as well as client or patron, of numerous artistic projects.

DATA
TEXTILE INDUSTRY IN CATALONIA

The textile industry was pioneering in its use of steam machinery.

Textile mills:	Manual	Mechanical
1841	24.880	231
1850	24.008	5.580
1861	12.026	9.695

A new religious impetus
Josep Maria Bocabella's religious fervour wasn't an isolated case as towards the end of the 19th century Catalonia was experiencing a period of great spirituality, coinciding with the millennium celebration of the monastery of Montserrat (1880) and the proclamation of its Virgin as Patron of Catalonia the following year.

1881
IS THE YEAR
when the Virgin of the Monastery of Montserrat is declared Patron Saint of Catalonia.

1874
Cezanne sells his first painting *Maison de Pendu*
The artist was ignored in his time and hardly ever exhibited.

1875
Alfonso XII King of Spain
Exiled from the age of 11, he recovered the throne for the Bourbons.

1879
Edison invents the electric bulb
This invention led to the generalization of electrical illumination.

The location of the temple
Communion between architecture and urbanisation

Josep Maria Bocabella conceived the Sagrada Familia as an expiatory temple, in other words, financed by the alms of the faithful. He himself searched for donations in order to buy a centrally located plot of land in the Eixample, but his limited budget obliged him to look elsewhere: In 1881 the site of the future temple was paid for with the 172,000 pesetas (1.034 euros) he had accumulated under the floor tiles of his bookstore.

The city expands

Sagrada Familia was witness to the expansion of Barcelona. At the beginning of the 19th century the city was experiencing an unprecedented demographic explosion. The growing industry attracted thousands of workers to the city which, surrounded by an ancient wall, could no longer hold all its inhabitants. The sanitary situation was very poor and the cholera epidemic in 1854 hastened the decision to demolish the walls which was carried out between 1854 and 1856.

The Sagrada Familia temple in 1928
This photograph shows what the temple's surroundings were like in 1928. When work commenced, this area of the Eixample was far away from the centre and was a neighbourhood still in construction and inhabited by labourers.

DATA
INHABITANTS OF BARCELONA

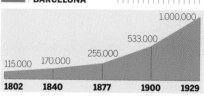

1.000.000
533.000
255.000
115.000   170.000

1802	1840	1877	1900	1929

CHRONOLOGY
KEY FACTS ABOUT GAUDÍ'S PERIOD

1883
The Chicago School. After the city fire in 1871, construction commenced on numerous skyscrapers.

1887
The automobile is born. Karl Benz and Gottlieb Daimler boosted the automobile industry with the combustion motor.

1888
Foundation of the UGT union
This trade union influenced by Marxist ideology emerged in Barcelona.

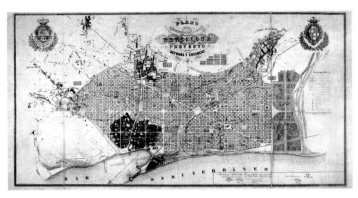

The Eixample project
Barcelona's magnificent urban expansion project contributed to the creation of a more egalitarian city. It was devised that every zone would have all the services that the citizen required.

Cerdá, the creator of the Eixample
Architect and town planner, he encountered many obstacles at the start of the project, but little by little managed to convince the sceptics.

The Barcelona Eixample

Bocabella was convinced from the start that Sagrada Familia had to be situated in the Eixample. This urban development project, devised by the engineer Ildefons Cerdá, was approved in 1859 and consisted of a great network of perpendicular and traversing streets. The blocks weren't squared but had bevelled edged corners (chamfers) which facilitated visibility. In each block, building on only two sides was permitted so that the rest could be dedicated to gardens. Cerdá also planned that the neighbourhood would possess communitary services such as a school, a civic centre and a market. All in all, it was a project for an egalitarian city designed to be enjoyed by its inhabitants.

DATA
MEASUREMENTS OF THE NEW EIXAMPLE

Approximate area	1.500 ha
Block measurement	113 x 113 m
Surface area of block	1,24 ha
Width of pavement	5 m
Width of road	10 m
Height of buildings	16 m

1894
Invention of the radio. The Italian Guglielmo Marconi was the first person who managed to transmit radio signals.

1895
First cinema projection
Took place in Paris, organised by its inventors, the Lumière brothers.

1898
Independence of Cuba. After its defeat in the war against the United States, Spain lost the colony of Cuba.

1899
Foundation of F.C. Barcelona
A Swiss residing in Barcelona, Johan Camper was founder of the football club.

The first stone is laid

A temple is born with the stamp of the neo-gothic style

The official date of birth of the temple of the Sagrada Familia is the 19th of March 1882, falling on the festival of Saint Joseph. The laying of the first stone was a great public event which was at-tended by all of Barcelona's civil and ecclesiastical authorities. This first stone was to serve as the base for the temple projected by Sagrada Familia's first architect, Francisco del Villar.

Francisco del Villar's project

When Bocabella ruled out the idea of reproducing the Loreto basilica, he entrusted the project to Francisco del Villar, a diocesan architect who in 1877 had offered his services free of charge to work on the plans for the new temple. Del Villar planned a neo-gothic church, the style in fashion for religious architecture and his project consisted of a church with three naves, a large-sized crypt and a high needle-shaped bell tower.

Del Villar the architect
This diocesan architect devised the initial project and was at the helm of building work on the Sagrada Familia until his resignation in 1883.

1882

WAS THE YEAR when the first stone was laid. After the ceremony, work was started on the construction of the crypt.

 CHRONOLOGY
KEY FACTS ABOUT GAUDÍ'S PERIOD

1900
First zeppelin flight. The German Count Ferdinand von Zeppelin invented this aircraft lighter than air.

1900
Freud publishes *The Interpretation of Dreams* This book sets out the basis for the theory of psychoanalysis.

1903
First piloted flight The brothers Wilbur and Orville Wright invented the first aeroplane propelled by an engine.

Original drawing of the project by the architect Del Villar
Francisco del Villar planned a temple with elements typical of the neo-gothic period such as large honeycomb windows, exterior buttresses and a high needle shaped campanile.

The façade
The most characteristic elements of the first façade planned for the temple are the bell tower, the large windows and the access stairs with their five entrance-ways.

Del Villar's resignation

Del Villar's position in the project turned out to be ephemeral. Shortly after the supporting pillars of the crypt had been built, discrepancies commenced between Del Villar and Josep Maria Bocabella's technical assessor. Del Villar planned to build the columns with blocks cut from solid stone, while the management defended a much more economical system which consisted of erecting pillars with pieces of stone on the inside and outside which would later be filled in with masonry. The differences ended up being definitive and in 1883 Bocabella accepted Del Villar's resignation, fearful of remaining without funds to continue the project.

The first stone
The ceremony to mark the laying of the first stone was a great public event and had huge press coverage.

1905
Einstein announces the theory of relativity
The German scientist revolutionized the classical concepts of physics.

1908
Auguste Rodin sculpts The Kiss
This sculpture, along with The Thinker, is one of this French sculptor's most famous works.

1911
Amudsen arrives at the South Pole
The Norwegian explorer was the first man to reach the South Pole.

1914
First World War
Known as the Great War, it lasted until 1918 and involved 32 countries.

Gaudí takes over

The arrival of the architect breathes new life into the temple

After Francisco del Villar's resignation, Bocabella offered control of the building work to his technical assessor, who declined but proposed one of his collaborators, Antoni Gaudí, to lead the project. It was the year 1883 and Gaudí was a young architect who at the age of 31 had already demonstrated excellent qualities. Quickly, Gaudí went beyond the original project and transformed it into a universal masterpiece.

Gaudí's first interventions

Enthused about the project, Antoni Gaudí officially became the temple's architect on the third of November, 1883. At that time, construction on the crypt's pillars, designed by Del Villar, had already begun and one of the first things that Gaudí did, was to transform them, providing them with naturalistic capitals. In 1884, the first plans of Sagrada Familia to be signed by Gaudí were for the design of the Chapel of Saint Joseph, situated in the temple crypt. Its construction was rapid and mass was first held at its altar on the 19th of March, 1885. Nonetheless, the crypt wasn't finished until 1891, with a few of the chapels still remaining to be decorated.

Antoni Gaudí
When he took charge of the Sagrada Familia project in 1883, Gaudí was a young architect with little work constructed, but was already well-known for his enormous energy and originality.

CHRONOLOGY
KEY FACTS ABOUT GAUDÍ'S PERIOD

1916
Birth of Dadaism
This artistic movement emerged as a criticism of western culture.

1917
The Russian Revolution. After overthrowing the Tsar, Russia became a Soviet state. Lenin was its first president.

1918
The Great War ends. German surrender meant the end of the war, in which almost 50 million people died.

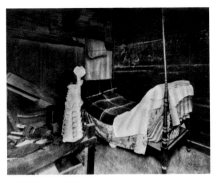
Gaudí's bed in the temple studio

Antoni Gaudí shows work on the temple

Gaudí's stamp

Shortly after taking on the project, Gaudí made an initial plan of the temple. This plan was limited by the crypt base, which had been built according to the original project, and he couldn't carry out all the changes he would have liked. One of these consisted in raising the temple in diagonal direction, to fully orientate the Nativity façade towards the sunrise and the Passion façade towards the sunset.

Plaça Reial lamp post
In Modernist style, commissioned by the City Council, Gaudí designed these street lamps.

The biography of a genius

1852
Gaudí is born in the province of Tarragona.

1868
He moves to Barcelona to study architecture.

1875
Begins military service in the Armed Infantry of Barcelona.

1876
His mother dies.

1878
He finishes architectural studies. He designs the lamp posts for Plaça Reial and the Pla del Palau commissioned by the City Council. He meets Eusebi Güell who becomes his friend and patron. He exhibits in the Universal Exhibition held in Paris in 1878.

1883
Commences work on The Caprice, in Comillas and Casa Vincens in Barcelona. He leads the building project of the Sagrada Família.

1886
Starts on the construction of Güell Palace.

1900
The Casa Calvet, is awarded the prize for best building by the City Council.

Work commences on Park Güell.

1904
He receives the commission to remodel the Casa Batlló.

1905
Pere Milà entrusts him with the construction of his home: La Pedrera.

1906
He moves to a house in Park Güell with his father and niece. Months after, his father dies at the age of 93.

1910
Commission of hotel in New York.

1911
Ill with maltese fever and then moves to Puigcerdà, where he draws up his will.

1912
His niece dies.

1914
Construction work on Park Güell is held up.

1918
His great friend and patron Eusebi Güell dies.

1925
He moves into Sagrada Família.

1926
On the 7th of July he is knocked down by a tram. Three days later, he dies in the Santa Cruz hospital, aged 74.

1919
Gropius founds the Bauhaus
This German architectural school was one of the most influential of modern art.

1922
Mussolini, head of government
After the so-called March on Rome, the Fascists take control in Italy.

1923
Dictatorship of Primo de Rivera
This military man headed the coup d'état and controlled Spain until 1930.

1926
Television is invented. The Scot John Logie Baird was the first person who managed to transmit moving images.

GAUDÍ'S MOST OUTSTANDING WORKS

Universal and innovative, Gaudí left an architectural legacy which continues to captivate for the originality of its technical and aesthetic resources.

Gaudí walking in Park Güell

Temple of the Sagrada Familia
A synthesis of his career, it was his most outstanding work, which he was dedicated to until he died.

Casa Vicens
Built between 1883 and 1888, it was Gaudí's first important project.

Episcopal palace
The residence of the Bishop of Astorga (Leon) is in keeping with neo-gothic style.

Finca Güell
It was his first commission by Eusebi Güell, and it is located in the city of Barcelona.

1883	1884	1885	1888	1889	1890	1892

The Caprice
Gaudí endowed this house with the Middle Ages style and the ostentation of oriental palaces. It is located near Santander.

Güell Palace
A work of great sobriety and situated in the heart of Barcelona.

Casa de los Botines
Located in León, this building is a clear exponent of Gaudí's gothic period.

The Teresian College
Place of study in Barcelona.

La Pedrera
Another masterpiece by Gaudí which stands out for its sinuous façade and chimneys.

Casa Batlló
Exceptional example of Gaudí's organic architecture. Over the polychromatic façade the balconies appear to hang like bird nests.

Güell Colony church
Only the crypt was built, to which Gaudí applied numerous technical innovations.

1895	1898	1900	1906	1907	1909	1914

The Güell wine cellars
Is in Garraf, a town near Barcelona.

Casa Calvet
Gaudí gave it a refined and sober air. It was awarded prize for the best building of 1900, by the City Council.

Park Güell
It was planned as a city garden. Gaudí incorporated architectonic elements, decorative and naturalist, with the Barcelona countryside as backdrop.

Bellesguard
In this country home Gaudí wanted to recall the glorious past of Catalonia in the Middle Ages.

02

GAUDÍ'S PROJECT

In search of the perfect temple

Antoni Gaudí gathered together all the symbols of Christianity in the temple of the Sagrada Familia.

In the commission of the temple of the Sagrada Familia, Antoni Gaudí took the opportunity to explore all of its architectonic potential and to achieve what no other architect had managed before him: the construction of the perfect temple. With this objective, he concentrated all his efforts on ensuring that the whole of the temple would be in perfect consonance with his final mission, which was none other than the celebration of liturgical rites. He therefore drew on all his innovative artistic and architectonic resources so that they would be perfectly adapted to the practice of religious cult. With the passing of the years and propelled by his anxiety for perfection, Gaudí was accumulating a sound religious knowledge along with a growing faith. As a result, he became an expert in liturgical themes, which is reflected in every corner of the temple.

Gaudí envisaged the Sagrada Familia as a Bible made of stone, which told the history and mysteries of the Christian faith. On the exterior of the temple he represented the Church, through apostles, evangelists, the Virgin and the saints. The cross which tops the main tower symbolises the triumph of Jesus's church and the façades evoke three crucial moments in Christ's life: his birth, death and resurrection. The interior refers to the universal church and the crossing, to the Celestial Jerusalem, mystic symbol of peace. All in all, Gaudí managed to combine his faith and his artistic genius to convert the Sagrada Familia temple into a universal masterpiece.

Gaudí, aged 36

Gaudí's Temple

A unique project. With Gaudí in charge of the construction work, Sagrada Familia was acquiring greater significance, as much for its revolutionary structure, as its complex symbolism.

Location and surroundings

Gaudí wanted Sagrada Familia to become a focal point. He therefore devised an urban development plan which consisted of a 8 pointed star-shaped square. This design enabled the viewer to observe from his angle of vision, the central cimborio, measuring 170 metres high, and two façades at the same time. Due to the elevated cost of the land, Gaudí had to opt for a more restricted layout which consisted of a 4 pointed star.

The architect in front of his temple Gaudí shows the Infanta Paz how work is progressing on the temple.

 PROCESS
PROJECTS PRIOR TO THE TEMPLE

The temple of the Sagrada Familia was preceded by two other projects by Antoni Gaudí.

1892
The Tangier Missions
In this project, which was never built, the shape of the towers already stand out.

1898
The Güell Colony Crypt
In its church, Gaudí experimented with roofs, vaults and columns.

1902
Temple of the Sagrada Familia
Is the compendium of the experiments and innovations of earlier projects.

Second urban development plan's project by Gaudí. The 4 pointed star-shaped square allows the viewing of the temple's silhouette from all angles.

Angle of vision. The temple was designed taking into account how it would be viewed by the passers-by.

JESUS' TOWER
The highest tower. It is crowned with a 15 metre high cross.

VIRGIN MARY TOWER
Is located on the temple apse.

EVANGELIST TOWERS
Carry the symbols of the four evangelists: the Angel, the Ox, the Lion and the Eagle.

BELL TOWERS
Are dedicated to Jesus' twelve apostles. They reach 118 metres high.

SACRISTIES
There are two and they are located on both sides of the apse façade.

PASSION FAÇADE
Represents the suffering of the Passion of Christ.

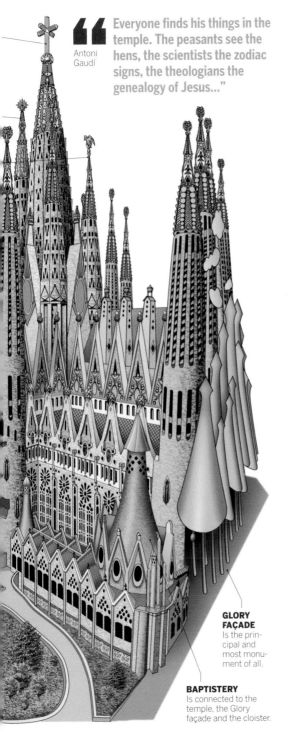

" Everyone finds his things in the temple. The peasants see the hens, the scientists the zodiac signs, the theologians the genealogy of Jesus..."

Antoni Gaudí

The sketches and models

Following the project's general concept, Gaudí made plans of the temple working on large sections. To resolve the technical problems which would occur, he used models, plans and drawings which he kept in his workshop. Unfortunately, during the uprising of 1936 the plans were burnt, but plaster models were preserved and restored after the Spanish Civil War.

Study of monument, 1902. To evaluate the aesthetic effect of shapes and volume, Gaudí used drawings.

The Passion façade, 1911
Gaudí used drawings and models to design the façades.

Models. So that he could visualize the temple better, Gaudí created models of the temple on a scale of 1:10 and 1:25.

GLORY FAÇADE
Is the principal and most monument of all.

BAPTISTERY
Is connected to the temple, the Glory façade and the cloister.

A monumental work

Closer to God. *The solemnity of the temple planned by Gaudí required enormous dimensions. Its numerous pinnacles and towers were nearer to heaven than any other building in the city.*

The ground plan

The temple of the Sagrada Familia is a building in the form of a Latin cross, measuring 94 metres long and 60 wide. The main nave is made up of 5 naves: a central one which is 15 metres wide and 45 metres high, and two lateral ones on both sides.

The arms of the cross correspond with two façades on the exterior: that of the Nativity and the Passion. There is a third façade, the Glory, situated at the start of the main nave. The apse, of lobular shape, is comprised of 7 chapels; below which a crypt is found.

View of the apse

Pinnacles
The towers are topped by pinnacles which are decorated with lively and bright polychromatic mosaics.

14.000
PEOPLE
is the total capacity which the temple interior will hold when liturgy is held.

4.500
SQUARE METRES
is the surface area taken up by the premises of the Sagrada Familia.

170
METRES
is the height of the central tower dedicated to Jesus, which for its symbolic importance is the highest of the temple.

ASSUMPTION CHAPEL
It will be devoted to the Assumption of the Virgin.

APSE

SACRISTIES
There are two placed on each side of the apse.

CLOISTER
Surrounds the collection of buildings which make up Sagrada Familia.

PASSION FAÇADE

BAPTISTERY

CRYPT
Located underground, it is the part of the temple which preserves more neo-gothic elements. At present it is the neighbourhood parish church.

The Nativity Façade. According to Gaudí's project, in order that the temple could be viewed easily, it had to be surrounded by garden and park areas.

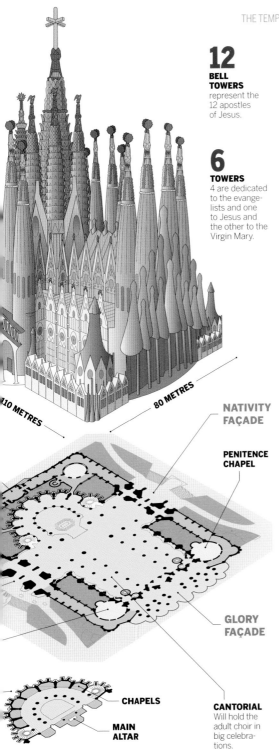

12
BELL TOWERS
represent the 12 apostles of Jesus.

6
TOWERS
4 are dedicated to the evangelists and one to Jesus and the other to the Virgin Mary.

110 METRES

80 METRES

NATIVITY FAÇADE

PENITENCE CHAPEL

GLORY FAÇADE

CHAPELS

MAIN ALTAR

CANTORIAL
Will hold the adult choir in big celebrations.

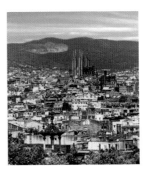

The height of the temple

With Sagrada Familia, Gaudí recovered the vertical anxiety that the churches of the Middle Ages had pursued. These constructions towered over the civil buildings, bestowing them with even more majesty and mysticism. Following this idea, Gaudí gave great ponderability to height in respect to the rest of the dimensions. The highest tower was dedicated to Jesus and reached 170 metres which meant that Gaudí could ensure visibility of his work from any viewpoint in the city.

COMPARISON
DIMENSIONS OF THE TEMPLE

The monument of the Sagrada Familia takes up an area similar to that of a large-sized football pitch (120 x 90 metres).

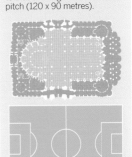

The structure

The global project. *In Sagrada Familia, Gaudí reunited and perfected the innovations and discoveries of his career as architect. For its structural conception, the temple represents the technical and artistic climax of its creator.*

Section of the naves
The columns are tilted to adapt to the stress trajectories. With this shape and its ramifications, the columns, despite their apparent fragility, can withstand all the load of the structure.

Proportion of the temple

Gaudí set out the temple under a general proportion, which is repeated throughout each part of the building. These proportions are based on one unit, half and thirds. For example, the interior of the temple measures 90 metres long (unit), 60 metres wide (two-thirds) on the transept and 45 metres wide (half) in the naves.

DATA MEASUREMENTS OF THE TEMPLE INTERIOR	
Width of naves	45 metres
Height of central nave	45 metres
Width of central nave	15 metres
Height of lateral nave	30 metres
Width of lateral nave	7,5 metres
Length of naves	90 metres
Between columns	7,5 metres
Width of transept	30 metres
Cross vault height	60 metres

The modulation of the temple
The modulation is the basis on which the temple is based and is used to establish the different proportions of the ground plan and the layout of the different elements which make it up.

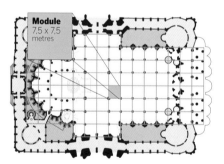

Module
7,5 x 7,5 metres

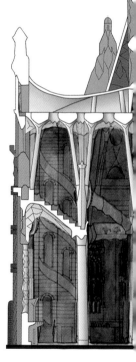

Gaudí's study. Gaudí fully dedicated the last years of his life to Sagrada Familia. This was the study where he worked. It is located on the site, along with the bedroom where he lived.

Revolutionary solution

Before Antoni Gaudí, Gothic architecture was the style which allowed the obtainment of great height with lighter support elements, but still required buttresses to sustain the structure from the outside. Gaudí wanted to dispense with buttresses and set about searching for technical

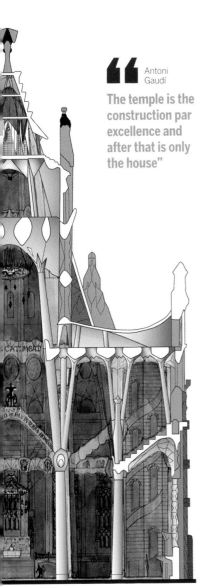

> Antoni
> Gaudí
>
> **The temple is the construction par excellence and after that is only the house"**

Calculation of the structure

First of all, Gaudí calculated the weight of the elements of the building. Later he built a model with strings, from which he hanged weighted bags to simulate the shape of the inverted building. The strings formed arches, called funiculars, which followed the strength lines of the structure. After, he would photograph them and turning the images around he would obtain the structure.

Funicular
By putting weights along the string, Gaudí's funicular arches were obtained.

Funicular model of the church of the Güell Colony
Before applying the catenary arch in Sagrada Familia, Gaudí developed this method in the Güell Colony.

 COMPARISON
NEW ARCH CREATED BY GAUDÍ

Romanesque arch
Withstands great loads but requires buttresses and thick walls to avoid collapse. For this reason only small windows are permitted.

Gothic arch
Allows great height and large windows for the entry of light, but still needs exterior buttresses so that the building doesn't collapse.

Gaudí's arch
The catenary arch or funicular allows the obtainment of great height and large windows without the need for buttresses, given that due to its shape it distributes the weight itself.

solutions that former styles hadn't found. Finally, he devised a new method. It consisted of studying the weights in order that the constructive elements were those that would be adapted to bear the load. From there evolved the curious shapes which the temple of the Sagrada Familia took on, with leaning columns and hyperboloid vaults.

Columns
The columns used by Gaudí are inspired by trees. They slightly tilt and branch out in the upper part to support the vaults.

THE SAGRADA FAMILIA AND OTHER TEMPLES

When work on Sagrada Familia is completely finished, its dimensions will exceed those of the most emblematic religious buildings.

70,66 METRES

Boeing 747. Is one of the largest aeroplanes in the world.

137 METRES

110 METRES

69 METRES

Nôtre Dame Cathedral
Paris

Archetypical of the medieval Gothic period, construction work commenced in 1160 and was completed in 1225.

Saint Paul's Cathedral
London

Built in 1710, it is one of the Anglican Church's most important temples.

Saint Peter's Basilica
The Vatican City

Construction commenced in 1506. Its design was the work of architects such as Bramante, Michelangelo and Bernini.

157 METRES

170 METRES

170
160
150
140
130
120
110
100
90
80
70

Cologne Cathedral
Cologne

Gaudí greatly admired this temple, which is considered to be one of the jewels of Gothic art. Work on it spanned more than six centuries: from 1248 to 1880. Within its interior lie the remains of the Three Wise Kings.

Temple of the Sagrada Familia
Barcelona

The Sagrada Familia will exceed in height the most representative temples. It is also one of the most spacious, as its surface area, 4.500 square metres, will be able to hold more than 14.000 worshippers.

01. The Passion façade (1960). Construction of the bell tower bases. **02. The apse (1893).** The exterior of the finished apse. **03. The Nativity façade (1897).** State of the work 5 years after their start. **04. Collocation of the Annunciation group.** Temple workers position the sculptures on the Nativity façade. **05. The Passion façade (1972).** The towers reach 55 metres. **06. The interior of temple.** View of the interior space of the temple during work on Passion façade. **07. Central portal of the Passion façade (1965).** The façade reaches 11 metres high. **08. The Sagrada Familia (1915).** View from the Hospital de Sant Pau. **09. Antoni Gaudí.** The architect with members of The Regionalist League.

03

The crypt

The first part of the temple that was built

The crypt is situated below the apse, between the Nativity and Passion façades. It was the first part of the temple that they started work on, when the project was still led by architect Francisco del Villar. A year after construction work had commenced, he resigned from his post. Antoni Gaudí took on the position and soon put his unmistakeable stamp of genius on to the neo-gothic crypt.

The revision of the neo-gothic style

The crypt, which in Greek means hidden place, is a temple space which brings to mind the catacombs or subterranean places where the first Christians hid in times of persecution. Gaudí took control of the construction of the temple when the raising of the crypt's columns had already commenced. The former project led by Del Villar was of pure neo-gothic style and Gaudí could only vary the elements which wouldn't affect the structure too much, such as raising the vault and adorning the capitals with naturalist details. He also surrounded the crypt with a deep ditch to prevent damp and, at the same time, to obtain illumination and direct and natural ventilation.

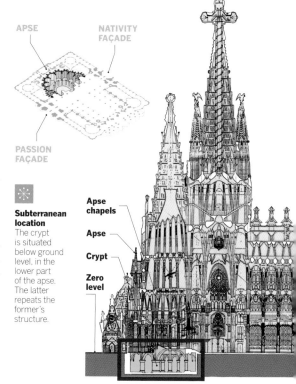

APSE

NATIVITY FAÇADE

PASSION FAÇADE

Subterranean location
The crypt is situated below ground level, in the lower part of the apse. The latter repeats the former's structure.

Apse chapels

Apse

Crypt

Zero level

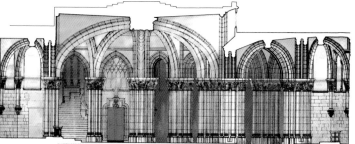

Section of the crypt
The central space is higher than the chapels. Thanks to this difference in height. Gaudí could open windows and naturally ventilate and illuminate the area.

The columns
Made up of 10 small pillars, each column supports the central crypt vault. Arguments over which material should be used to build them led to Del Villar's resignation.

Temple section
In the illustration are the different spaces proposed by Gaudí. In the lower part, the dimensions of the crypt can be observed.

The interior composition

The crypt is made up of seven chapels dedicated to the Holy Family of Jesus Christ which form a rotunda, in front of which are five other chapels in a straight line. Of these five chapels, the middle one houses the central altar, which is where mass is celebrated. According to what was originally planned, this central zone of the crypt will contain in the future, a reproduction of The Holy House of Nazareth, like the one venerated in Loreto.

3.619
DAYS OF WORK
was the length of time it took to build the crypt. Work commenced on the 19th of March 1882 and finished nine years later, in 1891.

Altar of The Holy House in Loreto

CHRONOLOGY
CONSTRUCTION OF THE CRYPT

1882
Construction commenced
The laying of the first stone was on the 19th of March. The same year excavation was completed.

1885
Work advances
The altar to Saint Joseph is finished, where mass is held despite the crypt being unfinished.

1936
The disasters of the Civil War
The three and only chapels that were finished were brutally destroyed in the year 1936.

The altar and the chapels

The crypt, where the remains of Gaudí and Josep Maria Bocabella lie, has twelve chapels dedicated to the Holy Family of Christ.

The apse chapels

The seven chapels which make up the semi-circle are dedicated to the Holy Family of Jesus. In the centre are the chapel of Saint Joseph, the Sacred Heart that represents Jesus' most human side, and that of the Immaculate Conception, dedicated to the Virgin Mary. Two other chapels are devoted to the Virgin's parents: Saint Joachim and Saint Anne. At one end, is the chapel of Saint John, Jesus' cousin, who was given the charge, at the Crucifixion, of looking after the Virgin Mary. At the opposite far end, is the chapel dedicated to Saint Elisabeth, Mary's cousin and Saint John's mother, and to her spouse Saint Zachariah.

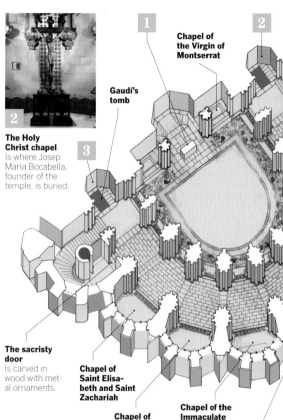

The Holy Christ chapel
Is where Josep Maria Bocabella, founder of the temple, is buried.

1 **Chapel of the Virgin of Montserrat**

2

Gaudí's tomb

3

The sacristy door
Is carved in wood with metal ornaments.

Chapel of Saint Elisabeth and Saint Zachariah

Chapel of Saint Joachim

Chapel of the Immaculate Conception

1885

WAS THE YEAR when the first mass was held. It took place on the 19th of March, at the Saint Joseph altar, when the crypt hadn't been covered over yet.

4

Chapel of Saint Joseph
It was the first one built, owing to the great devotion that Josep Maria Bocabella felt for Saint Joseph.

Lamps

Antoni Gaudí designed many of the lamps illuminating the crypt. Especially beautiful are those which light up the image of Saint Joseph.

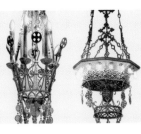

Holy water

The basin which holds the holy water is an enormous shell originating from the Philippines which Eusebi Güell gave as a gift to his great friend Gaudí.

Angel

The angels which seem to sustain the columns are inspired by the Apocalypse book.

Chapel of Saint John

Chapel of Saint Anne

Chapel of the Sacred Heart

 The central altar

Flanked by two chapels on each side, the central chapel holds the altar where mass is held at present. Presiding over it is an enormous relief representing the Holy Family.

3 **Chapel of Our Lady Carmen**

Gaudí wanted to be buried at the feet of this Virgin, to whom he was very devoted. His tombstone reads: *Antonius Gaudí Cornet, reusensis.*

The crypt relief

The Holy Family. Placed on the central altar, the relief that was originally on the altar of the Casa Batlló, is work of sculptor Josep Llimona. The design of the frame is by Antoni Gaudí.

The vaults

Gaudí combined mysticism, plastic beauty and ingenuity with technical solutions in the crypt's vaults.

The vault system

The crypt is covered over by a series of vaults supported by numerous Gothic style arches and columns. Each vault has a keystone or central stone on which different elements are sculpted. Gaudí modified Villar's project in order that the central vault, finished off with a great key stone representing the Annunciation, would be higher than the chapels. With this difference in height, he managed to add some small windows which gave better illumination and ventilation to the central nave.

Window

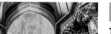

The keystone of the central vault
This polychromatic relief, a representation of the Annunciation by Flotats, was positioned by Gaudí at the point where the two large arches converge.

Mary
Kneeling down with crossed arms, demonstrates her submission and loyalty. Mary accepts the complex mission which God has in store for her.

The Holy Spirit
Embodied as a dove, the Holy Spirit is in charge of carrying out the mission of the conception so that the son of God is born unto Mary.

The Archangel Gabriel
The archangel acts as God's messenger and with decisive attitude, announces to Mary that she has been the chosen one to conceive Jesus.

Columns
Gaudí finished off the capitals with vegetable or naturalistic motifs.

" It isn't possible to go ahead without leaning on the past and taking advantage of the effort and achievements of the generations which precede us"

Antoni Gaudí

Polychromatism
The subtle golden decoration accentuates volume.

WHAT IS A KEYSTONE?
The keystone is an architectonic element which permits the finalizing of the nerves (continuations of the columns) in the highest part of a vault or in the middle of an arch. In the case of the crypt, these keystones are circular relieves of a high artistic value.

Plan of the crypt vaults
Around the central nave vault are 11 minor vaults. Moreover, each apse chapel is covered by a vault.

10
PILLARS
are those which support the central nave. They are formed by bunches of columns.

22
KEYSTONES
are found on the crypt vaults. Each one of them shows different images and symbols.

The keystone of wandering. An angel appears to emerge from the stone.

The keystone of the chapel of Saint Joseph. Represents Joseph's anagram.

Keystone of the chapel of the Immaculate Conception. It is Mary's anagram.

The keystone of the chapel of Saint Joachim and Saint Anne. Anagram.

01. Floor detail. Polychromatic mosaic depicting a bird feeding on a vine. **02. The Sacristy door.** Close-up of metallic ornamentation. **03. Chapel of the Immaculate Conception.** Sculpture of the Virgin of the chapel. **04. A detail from the Chapel of Saint Christ.** Stars in polychromatic mosaic. **05. Capital with vegetation details.** The leaves and other vegetation which cover the capitals were introduced by Gaudí in order to break with the strict neo-gothism of the crypt. **06, 07 and 08. Angels on the columns.** Are inspired by the Apocalypse book. There are 2, 4 or 6 winged ones. **09. Close-up of a window.** Image of an angel with trumpet announcing the Final Judgement.

05

06

07

08

09

04

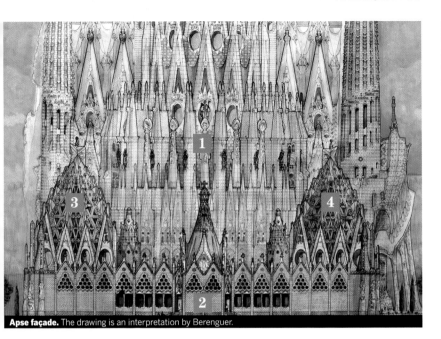

Apse façade. The drawing is an interpretation by Berenguer.

THE APSE FAÇADE

The monument dedicated to Mary

Gaudí was very devoted to the Virgin and for this reason he dedicated the apse tower and the Assumption chapel to her.

The series of constructions which make up the apse façade comprise of the mentioned apse which rises up as a majestic backdrop, the Assumption chapel, the two sacristies located on the sides, and the cloister which unites the chapel with the sacristies. In fact, the cloister designed by Gaudí surrounds the site, and helps unify the numerous constructions which make up the Sagrada Familia.

Gaudí also planned that on the cloister's intersections with each façade there would be a door dedicated to the Virgin. As an example he built the dedication to the Virgin of the Rosary, which he magnificently adorned with roses carved

in stone. The cult to the Virgin, which was instituted in the Catholic Church from the period of Concilio de Trento (1545-1563), reached its maximum splendour in the 19th century. This Marian fervour echoed in the field of the arts, as many artists dedicated their works to the veneration of the Virgin. Antoni Gaudí was also a great devotee to the Virgin Mary, as demonstrated by his wish to be buried in the chapel dedicated to the Virgin Carmen. For this reason, he believed it was essential to devote a significant part of the temple to the maternal figure of the Holy Family.

Salamander on the apse
1. Apse. **2.** Chapel of the Assumption.
3 y 4. Sacristies.

The apse

The perfecting of the Gothic

The apse is clearly Gothic inspired, like the crypt which it gets its structure from. Nonetheless, Gaudí's unique style is also apparent. He saw this architecture as "perfecting on the Gothic". On observing the gargoyles, windows and spires crowning it, nobody can doubt that he achieved this.

The temple grows

When the crypt was completed, Gaudí started work on the apse, whose position over the former meant it repeated its structure. Gaudí dedicated the apse and its tower to the Virgin, and all the symbols and images adorning it are based on liturgical verses dedicated to Mary. Nonetheless, the seven apse chapels commemorate the seven pains and pleasures of Saint Joseph, according to the wishes of the founder, Bocabella. It was not in vain that the devotion to Saint Joseph gave rise to the temple.

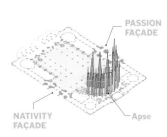

PASSION FAÇADE

NATIVITY FAÇADE

Apse

Saint Clare
On the apse there are sculptures dedicated to the founders of religious orders like Saint Clare.

Jesus' anagram
Jesus' initial is surrounded by a crown of thorns, which is a symbol of his martyrdom.

The Virgin's anagram
The crown situated over Mary's initial symbolizes her position as Queen of Heaven and Earth.

Saint Joseph's anagram
Joseph's initial is accompanied by narcissi, flowers which represent the purity and chastity of the saint.

> The projecting elements must be combined with the recesses, in such a way that each convex element, which is placed in full light, puts the other in shadow"
>
> Antoni Gaudí

3

Jesus' anagram
The letters *alfa* and *omega* recall that
Jesus is the Beginning and the End.

20.000
SCREWS
and 3.000 planks have been used
to put up the scaffolding used for
construction on the apse.

4

Earth and water snails
Indicate the position of the
spiral staircase.

Gaudí's first drawing of the apse
Gaudí based it on the Gothic style,
but lightened up its shapes.

The nature of stone

The apse exterior is a reflection of the great fascination that Antoni Gaudí held for nature.

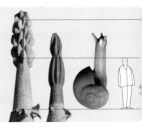

The naturalistic vision of Gaudí

Gaudí was a great observer of Nature. He had a deep admiration for all living beings and, in particular, plants and trees, which on numerous occasions were a source of inspiration in the aesthetic as well as technical sense. On one occasion he went so far as to say that his master was a tree which was growing near his workshop. Representations from the vegetable kingdom are frequent in his work, like the ears of wheat and floral motifs which top the pinnacles of the apse walls.

Wild herbs
The humble herbs growing on the temple grounds were depicted on the apse pinnacles.

Wheat ear
Gaudí chose wheat as a Eucharist symbol and for being a high quality Mediterranean cereal.

CHRONOLOGY
THREE YEARS OF CONSTRUCTION

1891 Just after finishing the crypt, Gaudí started work on the apse.

1892 After one year the exterior walls had been erected.

1892 Work advanced quickly; the walls reaching 19 metres high.

1893 Construction is completed on the apse exterior.

Dimensions
Gaudí calculated the dimensions of each element in order that they could be recognized a long distance away.

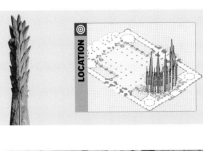

LOCATION

The gargoyles. These architectonic elements first used in the Gothic period have the function of draining away water accumulated on the roofs of the buildings.

The serpent
Biblical symbol of temptation and perfidy, the serpent appears to slide downwards.

WHAT IS A GARGOYLE?
It is the protruding part of a drainpipe which rainwater escapes down. In Gothic architecture they were often adorned with grotesque figures.

The animals

In the Gothic period, gargoyles were fantastical and demonic beings. Gaudí preferred to use common animals which were traditionally associated with evil. The amphibians and reptiles on the walls are not allowed to enter the temple. All are head down, fleeing from the purity radiating from Mary's symbols.

DATA
COMMON ANIMALS ON THE APSE

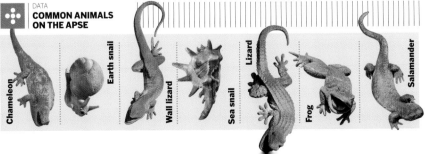

Chameleon · Earth snail · Wall lizard · Sea snail · Lizard · Frog · Salamander

The Cloister

Is designed to isolate the temple from the outside

Another of Gaudí's innovations was to recuperate the real significance of the cloister, which was meant to enclose. In monasteries and cathedrals, the cloister is located on one side and is used to provide access to other buildings. Gaudí's cloister surrounds the Sagrada Familia temple and is not only a place for prayer and religious processions, but also prevents street noise from entering.

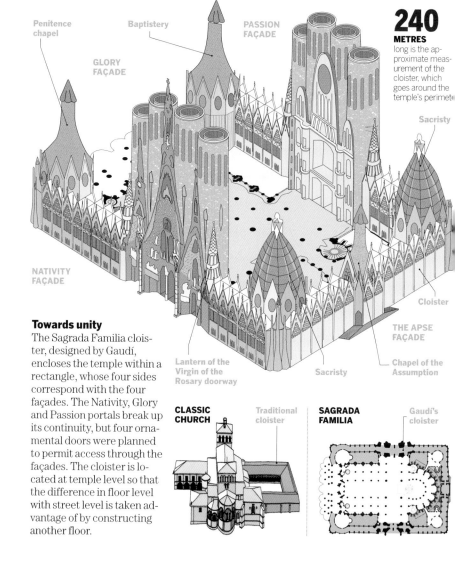

Penitence chapel

Baptistery

GLORY FAÇADE

PASSION FAÇADE

240
METRES
long is the approximate measurement of the cloister, which goes around the temple's perimeter

Sacristy

NATIVITY FAÇADE

Cloister

THE APSE FAÇADE

Lantern of the Virgin of the Rosary doorway

Sacristy

Chapel of the Assumption

CLASSIC CHURCH — Traditional cloister

SAGRADA FAMILIA — Gaudí's cloister

Towards unity

The Sagrada Familia cloister, designed by Gaudí, encloses the temple within a rectangle, whose four sides correspond with the four façades. The Nativity, Glory and Passion portals break up its continuity, but four ornamental doors were planned to permit access through the façades. The cloister is located at temple level so that the difference in floor level with street level is taken advantage of by constructing another floor.

1

2

The vault key stone Finely sculpted with great precision, this angel is depicted playing with sea foam he has lifted up with his own movements.

The Holy Family. This symbol is comprised of Jesus' cross, Joseph the carpenter's saw, and Mary's initial.

3

Mary's emblem In this window's keystone is the anagram which is typical in the representation of the Virgin Mary: her initial and the ducal crown.

The glass windows In the upper part of the cloister there is a numerous quantity of circular windows which are decorated with colourful motifs.

1890
THE FIRST SOLUTION FOR THE WALLS
Gaudí planned the walls with frontons decorated with rose windows, which would hold stained glass at a later date.

1919
THE SECOND SOLUTION FOR THE WALLS
Gaudí simplified the windows by making an equilateral triangle comprised of ten circular holes.

The Rosary Portal

Gaudí chose the Rosary portal to show how the decoration in the rest of the temple should be.

A doorway full of roses

Each cloister intersection with a façade gives rise to a door dedicated to the Virgin. Those that are situated on both sides of the Nativity façade are dedicated to the Montserrat and Rosary Virgin. On the Passion façade, are the Virgin de la Merced and Virgin de las Dolores. On the Rosary one, the cupola stands out illuminating all the doorway. All the architectonic elements, such as walls, vaults and arches, are decorated with a multitude of roses sculpted in stone with the precision of bobbin lace.

 1

Rosaries
The walls are decorated with rosaries which are sculpted with great realism.

2

The Death of Just. The Virgin shows the child Jesus to a man to help alleviate his pain.

The cupola
Despite its small dimensions, the portal is extremely well illuminated thanks to its cupola.

 3

The temptation of woman
A diabolical monster with fish-like form tries tempting a woman with a bag of money: it is the representation of vanity.

Virgin of the Rosary
The portal is presided over by the Virgin with child. At their sides are Saint Domingo and Saint Catalina.

Rose decoration
The explosion o f oses which flood the portal come from the figure of the Virgin of the Rosary.

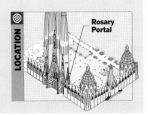

Rosary Portal

LOCATION

Phrases from the cloister cupola
Amongst olive leaves the last words of the Ave Maria are sculpted :
"*Et in hora mortis nostrae, Amen*".

5

The temptation of Man
Symbolic of violence, a demon offers an Orsini bomb to a worker. It was used by anarchists of the period.

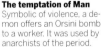

4

Isaac and Jacob
On each side of the door are sculptures of figures from the Old Testament: The kings David and Solomon and the prophets Isaac and Jacob.

 WHAT IS A LANTERN?
It is a small tower, higher than it is wide, with windows. It is used as a termination in buildings and churches.

The Assumption chapel and the sacristies

Both projects are distinguished by their original architecture

For the stretch of cloister which runs along the north wing of the temple, Gaudí planned a temple dedicated to the Assumption of the Virgin and two large sacristies situated on the vertices. These buildings contain a heavy symbolic load and the unmistakeable stamp of their creator: the chapel is like an enormous bed of stone and the sacristies have an original twelve-sided cupola.

Assumption Chapel

In the central part of the cloister on the apse façade, a small chapel is raised dedicated to the Assumption of the Virgin, popularly known as the August Virgin. Her festivity is widely spread in Catalonia and her bed, which is paraded around the streets in the procession of the Virgin of the Cathedral of Girona, inspired Gaudí in his design of the chapel: in which he reproduced all the elements which the bed is comprised of: the curtains, the crown, the pillars and the angels.

PASSION FAÇADE

NATIVITY FAÇADE

Assumption chapel

Sacristy

The project
30 metres high, the lantern is topped with a crown and its four sides are finished off with angels. The façade is presided over by the Virgin.

Drawing of the chapel. Original by Antoni Gaudí.

The Assumption. The August Virgin in Girona cathedral is by the sculptor Bonifàs and inspired Gaudí in the design of the chapel.

The sacristies

Gaudí positioned the sacristies on either side of the Chapel of the Assumption. They comprise of twelve-sided buildings, which are covered over by a cupola and perforated by triangular windows. These windows, along with twelve rose windows in the gallery frontons, guaranteed Gaudí an excellent illumination in the interior.

The symbolism

The cupola is decorated with mosaics and palms and finished off with a figure of a grape picker and a lamb, symbols of Jesus Christ.

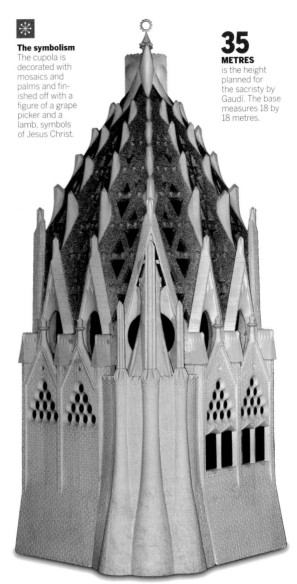

35
METRES
is the height planned for the sacristy by Gaudí. The base measures 18 by 18 metres.

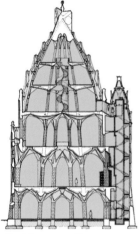

Sacristy cross section
Gaudí planned the sacristies to reach the height of 6 floors.

The obelisks
In each corner of the temple there will be three obelisks: each trio symbolizing a cardinal point, a cardinal virtue and a Christian fasting.

The plan view solution
Gaudí engraved the drawing of the plan view on a stone in order to carry out studies on the sacristy.

Plan view 1923
Definitive solution of the plan view.

Cupola
A horizontal projection of the cupola.

01. Apse pinnacle. On the stone of one of the apse pinnacles Jesus' symbol is represented. Behind it contrast the letters from one of the Nativity façade bell towers. **02. Cloister vault.** Gaudí's neo-gothic symmetry is clearly evident on one of the cloister's vaults. **03. Rosary Portal.** A generous decoration of roses sculpted in stone go around the doorway which allows access from the cloister to the Nativity façade. **04. Apse gargoyle.** A frog runs down the apse, fleeing from the purity radiating from Mary's symbols. **05. Cloister.** The second solution for the cloister, which Gaudí refined in 1919, had purer and more geometric forms.

05

The birth of Jesus. Sculpted group in the Charity Portal.

NATIVITY FAÇADE

The triumph of life

Gaudí depicted the most human side of Jesus and celebrated his birth with the exultance of Nature.

The Nativity Façade is also called *La Vida* (Life), *el Gozo* (Joy) and *La Navidad* (Christmas), given that it is an explosion of happiness on Jesus' birth. The stone seems to have lost its static character to convey the triumph of life with its own original forms.

This great stone nativity scene carries the message of Hope: Jesus has been born, "Saviour of Mankind". Nature is therefore shown in all her splendour and effervescence, as Jesus' birth means the liberation of all forms of life. As well as his birth, the main events in Jesus' childhood and adolescence are depicted on the façade: from the Annunciation up to his conversation with the scholars about the Holy Scriptures, on to the flight to Egypt or his appearance in the Temple, amongst others.

The whole of the façade exudes great tenderness, particularly in its depiction of the most human and family facets of Jesus, such as when he worked alongside Saint Joseph in his carpentry workshop. In order to create a sensation of proximity and naivety, Gaudí turned to popular elements, such as domestic animals and tools, which the public could easily relate to.

However, as with all of Gaudí's works, symbols of great complexity can also be found on this façade with which he tries to reach a higher transcendental plain.

Cockerel, Sculpture on the Faith Portal

The Nativity façade

Gaudí chose it to show off the potential of the temple

Antoni Gaudí wanted the Nativity façade to be the first one built so he could demonstrate all the plastic strength that could be achieved by the temple. Work on the foundations commenced in February, 1894 and spanned the first third of the 20th century. The façade was completely finished in 1930, when the four bell towers were raised.

The three porticos

The Nativity façade is comprised of three porticos and four bell towers. The porticos are dedicated to three theological virtues, which are each related to a member of the Holy Family. The central portico, the highest of all, is dedicated to Charity, whose maximum exponent is Jesus. The portico on the right-hand side is dedicated to Faith and devoted to Mary. Lastly, the portico on the left is that of Hope, whose best exponent was Saint Joseph. These three porticos form a unique monument which is set off by the three sculpted figures.

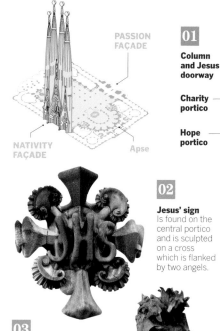

PASSION FAÇADE

NATIVITY FAÇADE

Apse

01
Column and Jesus doorway

Charity portico

Hope portico

02
Jesus' sign
Is found on the central portico and is sculpted on a cross which is flanked by two angels.

03
Mary's sign
Is on the Faith portico. As well as the initial M, this anagram contains a star, common symbol of the Virgin.

04
Joseph's sign
As patriarch and representative of the virtue of Hope, the anagram of Saint Joseph presides over this portico.

A model study. Gaudí planned that the façade would be painted in different colours.

The sculpture workshop
Gaudí and his team of sculptors did various studies and tests before definitively carrying out the structures.

Tree of Life
Is represented by a cypress, a symbol which can not be corrupted.

Faith portico

The sculptures
Gaudí took photographs to study the scenes to be represented. Once the model and posture had been chosen, a plaster cast was taken from the body. This process involved the collaboration of sculptors, Carles Maní, Llorenç Matamala and son Joan, amongst others.

Llorenç Matamala
This artist worked for years on sculptures with Gaudí.

 CHRONOLOGY
EVOLUTION OF A FAÇADE

1896
Work advances
Two years after the foundations are laid, the façade already has various columns erected.

1899
The porticos
In this year, only the upper part of the three portals remain to be built.

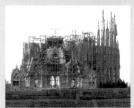

1920
Only the bell towers haven't been completed
The façade structure is finished and only the towers have to be finished off.

The Porticos

The three portals of the façade are separated by two columns which resemble enormous stone palm trees.

The columns

The two big columns that are separating the porticos are of great height and finely carved. On the base of each one there is a stone turtle, which symbolizes the unalterable and never changes with time. As for the shanks of the columns they are carved with upwardly spiralling grooves while the capitals are palm leaves from which surge bunches of dates covered in snow, acting as support to the four angel trumpeters who announce the Birth of the Baby Jesus to the four winds.

01

The chameleons
In contrast to the turtle and tortoise which represent permanence, on either side of the façade is a chameleon which symbolizes change.

?

WHAT DOES THE CHAMELEON SIGNIFY?
This reptile is known for its ability to change colour. It is therefore taken as a symbol of nature's constant transformation.

Angels and trumpeters
With their bronze trumpets, the angels announce the birth of Jesus.

05
Snow
In reference to the period of year when Jesus was born. Gaudí simulated icicles out of stone.

03
The column of Joseph
is the one which separates the Hope Portal (dedicated to Saint Joseph) from the Charity Portal (devoted to Jesus).

Palms
The capitals of the columns are formed by groups of palm leaves.

Joseph's inscription
Carved in stone, it is situated on the left column of the Charity portal.

Construction on the façade, in 1897
The construction work on the façade was carried out at the same time as the work on the sculptures which would be placed in their appropriate positions as time went on.

1899
THE ANGELS ARE PUT INTO PLACE
Trumpeters on the column's façade. Gaudí used models of three soldiers playing the trumpet. The fourth model was a collaborator of the architect.

The turtles
The column located on the mountain side is supported by a tortoise, while the coastal side is supported by a turtle.

04
Mary's column
Dedicated to the Virgin, it separates the Charity portico from the Faith Portico.

Turtle   **Tortoise**

The Charity portico

Simulating an enormous Nativity, the central portico, also called Love, is the largest on the façade.

09

The star of Bethlehem
This star surges out from the central group and its rays are focused on the child Jesus

06 The Coronation of Mary

Work by Joan Matamala, according to a project by Gaudí, represents the moment in which the Virgin is crowned as reward for her self-sacrificing love for God.

Jesus
Jesus blesses the Virgin Mary, and crowns her Queen and Empress of Heaven and Earth.

The Virgin Mary

Saint Joseph
In the Catholic tradition, the Holy Trinity crowns the Virgin. In this group, Saint Joseph substitutes God and a third man substitutes the Holy Spirit.

12

07 Zodiac signs

The constellations of the Zodiac are represented such as they were seen on the night Jesus was born.

08

Angel musicians
Three angels play classical musical instruments (harp, bassoon and violin), and three play popular musical instruments).

The lamb
Represents innocence and docility. It was a gift from the shepherds to Jesus.

The dog
As well as a popular illustration, it symbolises loyalty.

LOCATION

06

07

10

1

09

08

13

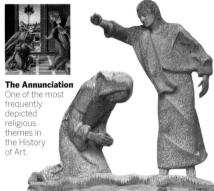

The Annunciation
One of the most frequently depicted religious themes in the History of Art.

10 The Annunciation of Mary

Shows the moment in which the Archangel Gabriel tells Mary that she has been chosen to be the mother of the son of God.

11

The rosary. The fifty-nine beads of the rosary go round the window.

Nature. Birds appear to be breaking out of the façade stone.

?

WHAT IS A ROSARY?
It is similar to a necklace. It has 59 beads which are used to recite the prayer by the same name.

12

The Adoration of the Kings. Melchior, Caspar and Balthazar, the Three Wise Men, offer their gifts to Jesus: gold, frankincense and myrrh.

13

The Adoration of the Shepherds
They were they were the first to see the star and worship the baby Jesus.

Column and doorway of Jesus

The Charity portico is divided by a pillar which acts as Jesus' genealogical tree and supports the representation of his birth.

1958
WAS THE YEAR when the sculpted group on the Nativity, by sculptor Joan Busquets, was put into place.

14 **The Nativity.** On the column's capital the recently born Jesus rests protected by Joseph and Mary. Like the homemade nativity models, there are also the ox and the ass.

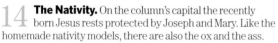

15 **Gloria in excelsis Deus...**
Inscribed in Latin on the upper part of the doors is, *"Glory to God on high and on earth peace to all men of goodwill"*, which is the phrase the angels said to the shepherds on the announcement of the birth of Jesus.

16 **Angel**
Just like the homemade nativity scenes, Gaudí placed the heralding angels over the manger

Choral angels
Around the manger, the angels sing in chorus to celebrate the birth of the son of God.

The sculptor Etsuro Sotoo
Dazzled by Antoni Gaudí's work, he has been collaborating with the sculptures on the Sagrada Familia since 1978.

LOCATION

18 The chorus of baby angels

The original sculptures were made of plaster and were destroyed during the Civil War. Those that can now be seen are an interpretation by sculptor Etsuro Sotoo, based on the ideas that Gaudí left behind.

Squirrel and flower. To reinforce the idea of happiness and triumph in life, nature is also represented.

19 The column of Jesus

In a ribbon wrapped around a column is the genealogy of Jesus. On the base there is a serpent biting the apple, symbolic of sin, which was the reason why Jesus came to Earth.

20

The inscription of Jesus

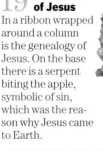

21

The snake and the apple

17

17

The phrase
The angels support an inscription which says *"Jesus est natus. Venite, adoremus."*

ANGELS WITHOUT WINGS
No angel on the Nativity Façade possesses wings, as Gaudí thought that angels couldn't fly.

The Hope portico

With this portico Gaudí reunited the childhood situations of Jesus which better embody Joseph and his virtue, hope.

Domestic animals
The geese or ducks on the lower part are an allusion to the Nile's fauna.

The Cave
Symbolizes refuge, Saint Joseph's attempt to protect the Church.

The anchor and the lamp
The large sized lamp, is used to light up the pathway of the Church.

The anagram of Saint Joseph
As well as its initial, the emblem is formed by bunches of grapes, irises and wood shavings.

22 Saint Joseph's boat
Saint Joseph appears as the helmsman who led the Catholic church, which is symbolized by the boat. The figure of Saint Joseph looks very much like Gaudí, given that, supposedly, it was the tribute which the temple workers paid to him after his death.

23

Jesus's family
Jesus shows an injured dove to his father, while his moved grandparents, Saint Joachim and Saint Anne, look on.

24 The flight to Egypt
The Holy Family fled to Egypt to avoid the death of Jesus at the hands of Herod's soldiers. An angel, energetically pulls on the ass which is ridden by the Virgin with the baby in her arms.

1935
THEY FINISHED
work on the last sculptures, completing work on the Hope portico that concluded 35 years of study and construction.

25 **The rocky outcrop of Montserrat**
The pinnacle which tops the portico seems to be an allegory of the mountain of Montserrat. Written on it is: *"Sálvanos"*.

LOCATION

26 **The betrothal of the Virgin Mary and Saint Joseph**

Mary and Joseph are shown at the moment when they are united in matrimony by a priest. There are also various angels present who assist in the ceremony.

Rosary and tools
Gaudí combined the holy (the rosary) with the everyday, personified by the great variety of tools sculpted.

27

28

29 **The Massacre of the Innocents**

With great dramatic force, this event is presented by a soldier of enormous dimensions who on the point of killing a new born baby is unperturbed by the pleading cries of its mother.

ANECDOTE
The real life model of the soldier had six toes on one of his feet. When Gaudí saw the sculpture he wanted to retain them to accentuate the monstrosity of the act.

28

29

The Faith portico

This portico is dedicated to the Faith and the Virgin Mary, as maximum exponent of this virtue.

30 **The Heart of Jesus**
The heart, the most human representation of Jesus, is covered by thorns and mystic bees which feed on his blood.

31

Joseph and Mary
With a mix of adoration and surprise, they observe their son while he explains to the doctors in the temple the exact sense of the Holy Scriptures.

32 **Jesus working**
A familiar scene from his years in Nazareth: Jesus helped his adoptive father in the carpenter's workshop.

Study of the sculpture
The figures were made in plaster before being sculpted.

33

The Visitation
The Virgin Mary visits her cousin Elisabeth to tell her that she is expecting the Messiah.

36

Providence
Divine Providence is represented by the hand that drives and the eye that sees.

LOCATION

34

The Immaculate Conception
Recalls the Catholic Church dogma which advocates that the Virgin was conceived without the original sin.

35

Mary's anagram
The initial of her name carries the star which identifies the Virgin.

37 Jesus in Simon's arms
Satisfying Hebrew law, Joseph and Mary present their child to the temple, where he is blessed by the priest Simon.

112 MEN
were the people who were working on the temple in 1897.

38

Wheat
The grapes and wheat symbolize the wine and bread shared out in the Eucharist.

39 Saint John the Baptist, Jesus and Zachariah
The figure on the right is Saint Zachariah, the father of Saint John the Baptist, Jesus' cousin, who is in the centre preaching in the temple.

37
39
32

Three pointed lamp
The Virgin's pedestal is a lamp whose three points symbolize the Holy Trinity.

The Tree of Life

The pinnacle is the symbolic compendium of the three porticos: it represents the triumph of life and the legacy of Jesus.

The dove
Represen
The Faith
who turn
God.

40 Jesus' anagram

The letters JHS which refer to Jesus Christ, are on a cross, on whose sides are the Greek letters *alfa* and *omega*. This anagram symbolizes that the Cross, in other words, Jesus, is the beginning and end of everything.

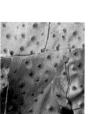

Incense
Jesus' anagram is surrounded by angels' incense.

?

WHY WAS JESUS' NAME ABBREVIATED TO JHS?
It comes from the name Jesuchristus. The *J* is the initial, the *H* is the middle letter and the *S* is the last letter in the word.

21
DOVES
are sheltered in the Tree of Life, all of them are sculpted in marble.

41 The pelican

Primitive Christian symbol, representing the Eucharist, as it was believed in Antiquity that this bird opened its chest to feed its chicks.

40

The Egg
Symbolises the origin and plenitude of Nature.

42

The cypress
This tree symbolises eternal life for its resistant wood and its evergreen leaves.

LOCATION

43 Holy Trinity
The pinnacle is crowned with the Greek letter *tau*, God's initial in the Greek language; with the cross, Jesus' symbol, and the dove which is identified with the Holy Spirit. In this manner, the Holy Trinity is represented.

Stairs
The two stairs leaning on the cypress represent aspiration to reach God.

44 Angels bearing wine and bread
In clear reference to the Eucharist, some angels collect Christ's blood to share it out to Humanity, while others are in charge of giving out bread.

45

The angel censers
Sign of purification, they scatter the sacred smoke with their censers.

THE CREATIVE PROCESS OF THE SCULPTURES

In order to bestow a great physical and psychological realism on to his figures, Gaudí meticulously studied the human body and created a new sculpture technique.

1 STUDY OF SKELETON

Gaudí considered the skeleton to be the base of sculpture, as it is the invariable part of the human body: which bestows character and appearance.

Skeleton studies

LIFE-LIKE DOLLS
Gaudí used some wire dolls to study the posture of the person to be represented.

Sketch of Jesus crucified (above) and angel (below).

2 PHOTOGRAPH OF MODELS

To achieve an overall view of the figures, Gaudí devised a system of mirrors, which showed the image of the model from all angles.

↑

Photography
The artist photographed the models and their reflections which he then studied in more detail.

↓

3 CASTING TECHNIQUE

After choosing the model and the posture it should adopt, Gaudí made a direct plaster cast from nude bodies of people and animals.

The flight to Egypt. Casts.

THE RAISED ASS
In order to execute the figure of the ass from *The Flight to Egypt*, Gaudí made a cast from a live ass. In order that the animal wouldn't move around he hoisted and suspended it in the air during the process.

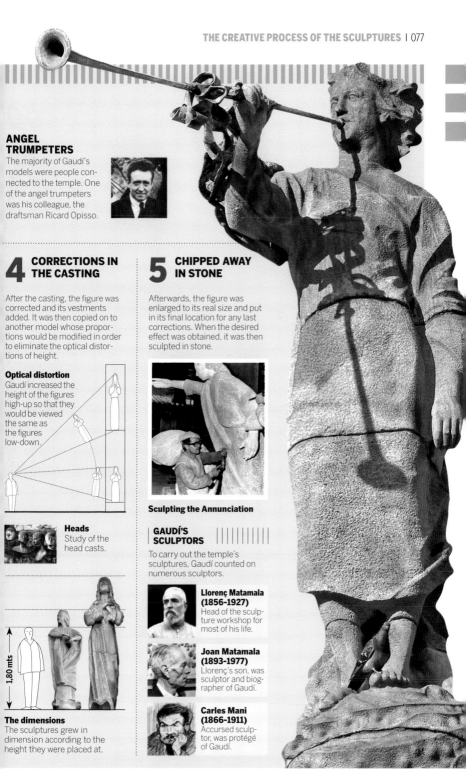

ANGEL TRUMPETERS

The majority of Gaudí's models were people connected to the temple. One of the angel trumpeters was his colleague, the draftsman Ricard Opisso.

4 CORRECTIONS IN THE CASTING

After the casting, the figure was corrected and its vestments added. It was then copied on to another model whose proportions would be modified in order to eliminate the optical distortions of height.

Optical distortion
Gaudí increased the height of the figures high-up so that they would be viewed the same as the figures low-down.

Heads
Study of the head casts.

The dimensions
The sculptures grew in dimension according to the height they were placed at.

1,80 mts

5 CHIPPED AWAY IN STONE

Afterwards, the figure was enlarged to its real size and put in its final location for any last corrections. When the desired effect was obtained, it was then sculpted in stone.

Sculpting the Annunciation

GAUDÍ'S SCULPTORS

To carry out the temple's sculptures, Gaudí counted on numerous sculptors.

Llorenç Matamala (1856-1927)
Head of the sculpture workshop for most of his life.

Joan Matamala (1893-1977)
Llorenç's son, was sculptor and biographer of Gaudí.

Carles Mani (1866-1911)
Accursed sculptor, was protégé of Gaudí.

07

01. Jesus carpenter. A young Jesus works in Joseph's workshop. **02. The Column of Jesus.** A ribbon wrapped around the column shows Jesus Christ's genealogy. **03. The shepherds' gift.** Jesus is born and is presented with a basket full of eggs. **04. Letter A.** Is one of the many typographical elements of the Nativity façade. **05. Jesus's monogram.** The signs JHS are worked in steel. **06. The adoration of Balthazar.** In a small chest he offers gold to the Holy Family. **07. The Zodiac.** Gaudí represented the Zodiac constellations as they were seen on the night Jesus was born. **08. The Birth of Jesus.** Mary protects the newly-born Jesus. **09. Angel chorus.** Numerous angels announced the arrival of the Messiah. **10. Birds of stone.** Flocks of birds free themselves from the stone. **11. Domestic animals.** A goose alludes to the fauna of the Nile. **12. Massacre of the Innocents.** A baby lays dead at the feet of a soldier. **13. The dove.** White doves shelter in the Tree of Life. **14. The adoration of Caspar.** In his bowl he brings incense on Jesus' birth.

06

Drawing of the Passion façade. Original by Gaudí, 1911.

THE PASSION FAÇADE

The representation of Death

Gaudí devised all the elements of the façade to reflect the suffering of the Passion of Christ.

On observation of the Passion façade one can't help feeling a certain sensation of coldness and sadness. For this is what it strives to do, to show Jesus' suffering (The Passion) and his death. Gaudí was conscious of the impact that this portal would have on the citizens, and it was why he decided to start building it once the Nativity façade had been completed. By doing so, he avoided popular rejection and gained more leeway in order that the global message of the temple would be understood. To convey this idea of desolation and pain, Gaudí freed the façade from any type of ornamentation. Likewise, he simplified its structure leaving clean and hard bone-like forms, with no more adornment than the cold nudity of the stone. The reason for this absence of decoration is so the viewer pays all his attention to the monument's group of sculptures which describe the last days of Jesus. All of the portal functions as an enormous stage in which the most relevant events in the Passion of Christ will chronologically unfold before the viewer's eyes. The Catalan artist Josep Maria Subirachs was responsible for carrying out the sculptures on this façade and he did so by interpreting the material that Gaudí left behind. His work is characterized by its angled and schematic forms, whose marked profiles help to underline the drama of the monument.

Soldier from the group *"The Veronica"*

The Passion façade

Pain and sacrifice sculpted in stone

In contrast to the optimism and vitality exuded by the decorative exuberance of the Nativity façade, the Passion expresses the pain of Christ's death with austerity and harshness. West-facing, where the sun sets, this façade recalls the cruelty of sacrifice through a series of sculpted groups which represent the last days of Christ.

The Passion according to Gaudí

In 1911, Gaudí withdrew to Puigcerdà to recuperate from a serious illness which was life-threatening. He was inspired by his own suffering and he set upon planning the Passion façade, where he wanted to imprint all the hardness of sacrifice. Gaudí left behind various drawings, studies and sketches on how the structure and decoration should be.

It was in 1954 that work commenced on the façade according to Gaudí's project, which consisted of a portico supported by six leaning columns, over which a great frontage is sustained by 18 small bone-shaped columns. This frontage is the last thing remaining to be built on all of the Passion façade monument.

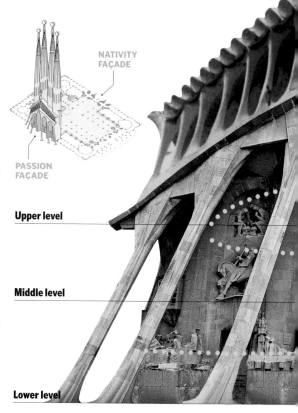

NATIVITY FAÇADE

PASSION FAÇADE

Upper level

Middle level

Lower level

CHRONOLOGY
THE EVOLUTION OF THE FAÇADE

1960

1965

1969

> " It could be that someone will find this façade too extravagant, but I wanted it to frighten, and on trying to do so I won't skimp on the chiaroscuro"

Antoni Gaudí

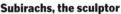

How to view the sculptures
The dotted line indicates the sequence to follow when viewing the sculptures.

Subirachs, the sculptor

In 1986, the artist Josep Maria Subirachs started on the execution of the sculptural groups on the façade. After dedicating a year to the study of Gaudí's work, Subirachs commenced sculpting in 1987 and from this moment, just like Gaudí did, he was fully dedicated to a task which has become the most important work of his life. As his sculptures show, Subirachs is defined as an extremely cerebral sculptor.

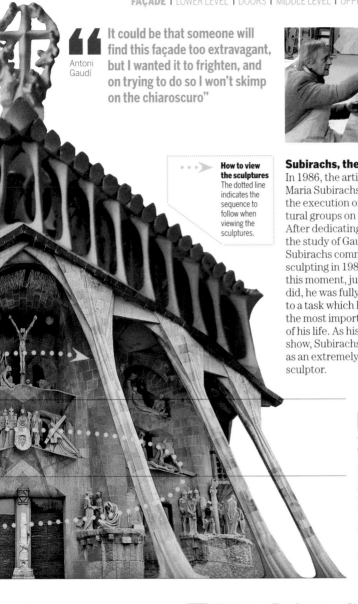

The Passion façade
The sculptor Subirachs made the order of the scenes, from the Last Supper to the Burial, follow an "S" shape to reproduce the path that Jesus followed on the road to Calvary.

Tree-like columns

To sustain the weight of the portico Gaudí dreamt up enormous leaning columns, similar to the trunk of the conifer tree, the sequoia. These monumental masses of stone, add to the monument's feeling of nudity and desolation.

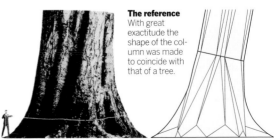

The reference
With great exactitude the shape of the column was made to coincide with that of a tree.

The lower level

Here immortalized are the events that happened the night before Christ's crucifixion.

The Roman eagle
Is situated on the column whose inscription reads: "Tiberius, emperor of Rome".

01 The Last Supper

Is the nearest group of sculptures. It represents the moment when Jesus, sitting at the table in the middle of the disciples, asks Judas to betray him as quickly as possible. The apostles are shown to be totally distressed.

02 Peter and the soldiers

Is the moment when Peter tries to prevent the soldiers from taking Christ.

The ear
In his struggle with the soldiers, Peter cuts off the High Priest's servant's ear. The apostle only abandons the struggle with the guard when Jesus tells him to.

03 The kiss of Judas

Sealing his betrayal, Judas kisses Jesus to indicate to the soldiers who his master is. This scene took place at night, hence the undefined outlines of the sculptures suggest how these people would have been viewed in the dark.

The serpent
Traditionally associated with evil and in this case being the devil's symbol that inspired the disciple to betray Christ. For this reason it is placed behind the figure of Judas.

The dog
Belongs to The Last Supper group. It is interpreted as loyalty or indifference to betrayal.

LOCATION

The cockerel
As was predicted, Peter denies that he knows Jesus, before the cockerel cries announcing the dawn of a new day.

04 The denial of Peter

The three women symbolize the three times that Peter denied knowledge of Jesus. The apostle appears wrapped in a sheet (metaphor of denial), ashamed by his cowardness.

05 Ecce Homo

After being beaten, Jesus is presented to the people wearing a crown of thorns.

06 The trial of Jesus

Pilate washes his hands, with this gesture the governor abstains from deciding Christ's destiny.

The labyrinth
It is a symbol recuperated from medieval cathedrals which recalls Jesus' path after his capture.

The cryptogram
It contains sixteen numbers. The sum of these, in 310 different combinations, always adds up to 33, Christ's age when he died.

The doors

The Gospel is present on the three doorways, while the image of the flagellation of Christ dominates the monument.

Alfa and omega
Are the first and last letters of the Greek alphabet and symbolize the beginning and end of creation

07 The Gospel Doors

Over the central door the gospel text is reproduced and narrates what the façade sculptures illustrate, the last two days of Jesus. This way, the doors function like the pages of a monumental New Testament, which serve as a background to the flagellation figure.

8.000
BRONZE CHARACTERS
Were cast to write the text on the door.

08 The flagellation

Christ's solitude during his flagellation is depicted by his position: this figure is placed between the denial of Peter and the betrayal of Judas. It is the most important sculpture on the lower level and is therefore five metres high and sculpted in travertine marble.

The fossil
According to the sculptor, a fossil of a palm leaf was found in the block of marble stone, symbolizing martyrdom.

The cane
Reflects the ridicule suffered by Jesus when the soldiers gave him a cane instead of a sceptre which symbolizes royalty.

The key
Is placed on the door of the Coronation of Thorns.

LOCATION

The column
Its division into four parts symbolizes the four arms of the cross. It's juxtaposition recalls the end of the ancient world.

The knot
Sculpted with great realism, the knot symbolises the physical torture suffered by Christ.

09 Door of Gethsemane

Represents, by relief and verse, the garden where Jesus prayed before being seized whilst his disciples were sleeping.

10 Door of the Coronation of Thorns

Shows the martyrdom of Christ. On its surface a quote from the Divine Comedy and some poems are engraved.

The middle level

Presided over by Christ's face stamped on the "Veronica", this level represents the path to the crucifixion.

Detail
This figure represents a girl from the group of women from Jerusalem that Jesus encountered on the way to the mountain of Calvary.

11 Longinus

Is believed to be the soldier that crossed his lance across Jesus' side on the cross. Afterwards, he converted to Christianity and ended up as a Church martyr.

12 The "Veronica" and the evangelist

Shows Jesus' second falter on the Calvary path. In the middle of the scene Veronica appears showing the veil on which Jesus' face is marked. Her figure has no face in order that more attention is paid to Jesus' face. Here, the sculptor, pays homage to Gaudí: by the evangelist and soldiers' helmets, which represent Casa Milà's chimneys.

13 The Three Marys and Simon the Cyrene

Jesus is shown fallen whilst Simon the Cyrene helps him carry the cross. The three crying women represent the Virgin, Mary of Cleophas and Mary Magdalene.

First sketch of the façade
Gaudí's first proposal for the Passion façade was very similar in structure and imagery to that of the Nativity façade.

LOCATION

Tribute to Gaudí. Subirachs used this photo as a base to represent Gaudí as the evangelist who would tell the story of Jesus.

La Pedrera. In another homage to Antoni Gaudí, Subirachs copied the Roman soldier helmets of the Pedrera chimneys.

Negative image. Is the sculptural way of representing the mark of Jesus' face on the veil that Veronica gave him to wipe away his sweat.

Upper level

This level represents, in a dramatic way, the death of Jesus on the cross and his burial in the tomb.

Nicodemus
This person helped Joseph of Arimatea to bury Jesus.

14 Soldiers playing dice

The soldiers play for Christ's clothes. The table is shaped like a lamb's bone, which was used to make the dice.

15 The crucifixion of Jesus

Jesus has now died on the cross. On his left are Mary Magdalene, kneeling, and the Virgin Mary, who is being consoled by John. A little further back is Mary of Cleophas. The cross is made with two iron bars. The front part of the start of the vertical bar is painted the colour red to highlight an "I", the first letter of the inscription I.N.R.I.

18
The moon
Solitary on one side, it represents the night.

19
The Death
Is represented by a solitary skull.

17 The burial

It is the last scene. Jesus' body, wrapped in a sheet, is deposited in the tomb by Joseph of Arimatea helped by Nicodemus. Mary kneels down at the tomb entrance.

The egg. Symbol of saintliness and resurrection.

DATA
SCALE OF THE ELEMENTS

1,80 m

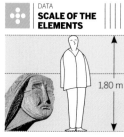

Drawing of the Passion
This is how the finished façade will look like, according to Berenguer.

LOCATION

16 The torn veil

This bronze structure represents the veil which separated the most sacred place in the Temple of Jerusalem from the rest of the large rooms. The upper arch of the atrium can be seen through, in which a series of inscriptions, letters and polychromatic drawings appear.

Veil detail. In order to achieve a similar effect to fabric, the bronze veil forms different creases.

Detail of the atrium. On the upper arch strong coloured letters and drawings are combined.

GETSEMANI

01. The flagellation of Jesus. Jesus is placed in front of the Gospel doors. **02. The Ascension of Christ.** Sculpted in bronze and weighing 2,000 kilos, it is placed on the bridge that connects the towers of Bartholomew and Thomas. **03. The horse of Longinus.** It is the horse whose master (according to tradition), crossed Jesus with his lance. **04. The lamb.** Done in brightly coloured ceramic work, it symbolizes the resurrection of Jesus. **05. The Coronation of thorns door.** The sculptor Subirachs used it to portray Jesus' suffering. **06. Pilate.** The Roman prosecutor is shown sitting next to Ecce Homo. **07. The secret meeting place.** Is located on either side of the façade. **08. The Last Supper.** The afflicted apostles at the exact moment when Jesus announces that he will be betrayed.

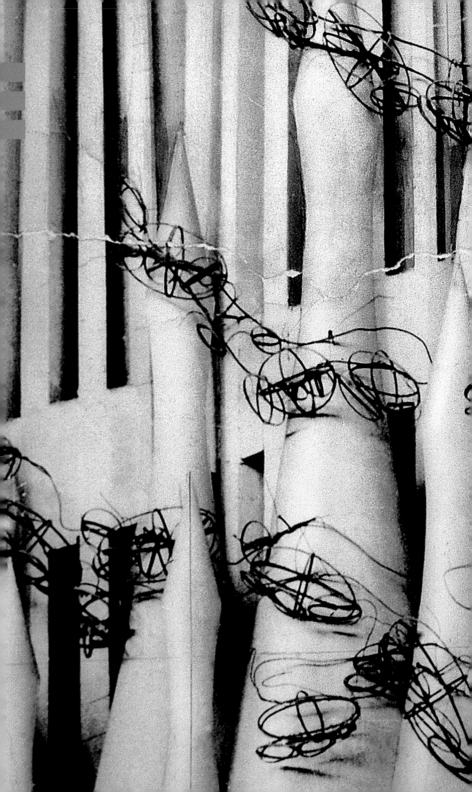

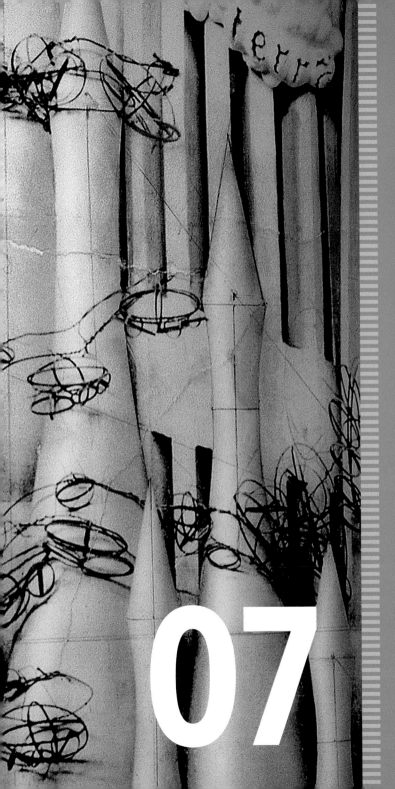

07

The Glory façade

The most important and monumental of all

The Glory façade will show Humanity's struggle to reach eternal life and each man's journey obtaining it. To do this, Gaudí wanted to represent Death, the first unavoidable step; the Final Judgement, presided over by Jesus Christ; the Glory, which is the reward to honourable men; and Hell, divine punishment which God inflicts on those who stray from his laws.

A spectacular entrance for the temple

Gaudí didn't tie up all the details of the Glory façade, but he did define, by means of a model, how its ground plan would be and the essence of its structure and its shape. Likewise, he also specified its symbolic and iconographic content which was highly complex and totally Gaudí. This façade is the monumental frame that Gaudí envisaged for the doorway which would allow access to the interior of the Sagrada Familia temple. His idea was that, before entering the holy area, the visitor would be conscious of how man was created and what his destiny is in this world. Over the doors, Gaudí imagined huge illuminated clouds which would hang from the bell towers and on which would appear the Creed in large letters: the prayer which sums up the dogma of Christian faith.

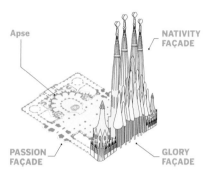

Apse

NATIVITY FAÇADE

PASSION FAÇADE

GLORY FAÇADE

The model made by Gaudí
The portico is covered by the four bell tower vaults and by sixteen lanterns, which are arranged in ascending order from the sides towards the centre and from the front to behind.

Bell Towers
Are the highest of the three façades. They represent Saint Peter, Saint Paul, Saint Andrew, and Saint James the Greater.

Jesus
To carry out the Final Judgement, Christ appears with attributes from the Passion, surrounded by angels.

Baptistery
Is decorated with allegories of baptism.

Death
According to the original project, death would be represented by tombs.

Entrance stairs to the temple
A staircase and terrace provide access to the Glory portico.

Antoni Gaudí

"Originality mustn't be sought for, as then it is extravagance. One must observe what is usually done and then try to improve on it"

The façade. Drawing by Berenguer.

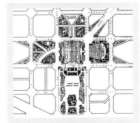

Montserrat. The doorway is inspired by the mountain Montserrat's curious forms.

The Creed
The letters of the word *Credo* (Creed) are luminous so that they can be read a long distance away at day or night.

16
LANTERNS of different sizes make up the portico.

Genesis
On the clouds which embrace the lanterns the creation of the world is narrated according to Genesis.

Penitence Chapel

DATA
URBANISATION STUDY IN THE YEAR 1975

The zone in the shape of a cross
According to a proposal in 1975, a garden would be in front of the Glory façade, reaching the Diagonal Avenue. At present, the City Council is working on other urban plans that differ to the cross shape proposal.

The Glory portal

On the Glory portal the history of man and all the pillars of the Christian faith are symbolized.

The portal's symbolism

On the façade every stage of Mankind is represented. Above the doors, are Adam and Eve, parents of humanity. Above them are Saint Joseph in his carpentry workshop, surrounded by workers. Higher up, are Faith, Hope and Charity, represented by the Ark of the Covenant, Noah's Ark and the House of Nazareth. The highest place of all, in the central axis, is reserved for the Virgin. Her gaze falls upon Jesus, who is judging Mankind. A great rose window symbolises the Holy Spirit and above it, at the highest point, soars the majestic image of God the Father.

The trumpeting angels and Noah's Ark are also represented on the portico.

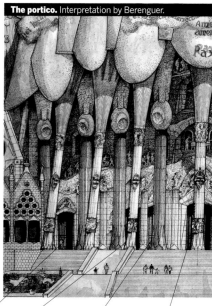

The portico. Interpretation by Berenguer.

The Baptism door
Its petition is: "Our Father who art in heaven, hallowed be thy name".

The Extreme Unction door
Is the rite which is given to the dying: "Come to us your Kingdom".

The Order door
Makes reference to the priesthood: "Thy will be done, on Earth as it is in Heaven".

The Eucharist door
Door which leads to the nave: "Give us today our daily bread".

The Glory, according to Titian
This is how the Renaissance painter imagined God's abode heaven, to be.

Columns and doors

To sustain the portico Gaudí planned seven exterior columns on which are inscribed the seven gifts from the Holy Spirit. On the base of the columns appear the Seven Deadly Sins and on the capitals, their opposite virtues. Each one of the seven doors which lead through to the temple is dedicated to a Church sacrament and to a petition of the Lord's Prayer. All the doors have different depths, as the wall is undulating. The most forward door will be the central one, which is subdivided into 3 doorways.

The most important façade
It takes up five naves and has the best position, as it is south facing.

 The construction of the Sagrada Familia is slow, because the Master of this work isn't in a hurry"

Antoni Gaudí

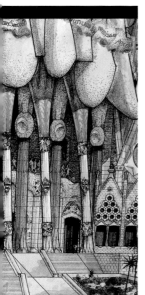

Monument to Fire and Water
Situated in the forecourt of the temple and in front of the Penitence chapel is a monumental torch with different arms, while at the other end, in front of the baptistery is a fountain which spurts water to a great height and represents the four rivers of paradise.

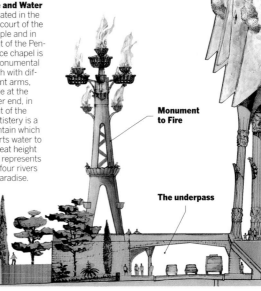

Monument to Fire

The underpass

 5°

The Confirmation door
"Forgive us our trespasses, as we forgive those who trespass against us".

 6°

The Matrimony door
The sacrament is matrimony and tells us: "Lead us not into temptation".

 7°

The Penitence door
Provides access to the Penitence chapel. It is related to: "Deliver us from evil".

The underpass
In Gaudí's original project, to obtain access to the Glory portal an enormous platform had to be built over the street Mallorca with steps on the other side of the street. This way, an underpass was created which would be in semi-darkness. Gaudí wanted to make the most of this lack of light in order to represent Hell. In this zone would appear demonic creatures, heresies, false gods, schisms, etc. Gaudí envisaged its style as oscillating between expressionism and popular art.

 PROCESS
THE CONCEPTION OF THE BAPTISTERY

By means of baptism, man purifies his sins and begins to form part of the Church and for this reason Gaudí gave the baptistery chapel a pre-eminent position on the façade. It has three doors: one connects with the street, another with the cloister and the last one, with the temple.

Drawing by Berenguer.

08

THE TEMPLE TOWERS

Touching heaven

Gaudí planned the temple exterior to be the most striking construction in the city.

In any period or civilization religious constructions have striven to differentiate themselves from other buildings by their shape and, above all, by their dimensions. Height bestows prestige and dignity upon a building which is in itself a mystic symbol, representing union with God.

Gaudí wanted his temple to be closer to heaven than any other building in Barcelona and therefore endowed its exterior with extraordinary dimensions. This monument is made up of eighteen towers whose heights are determined according to the hierarchical symbolism that they represent. Therefore, the central dome, the highest and most important, is the one which represents Jesus Christ and measures 170 metres high. Following in order of height, the tower dedicated to the Virgin Mary is 120 metres high, and then the four devoted to the evangelists reach 125 metres. Lastly, the twelve bell towers which represent the apostles serve as a backdrop to the three façades.

Their parabolic profile, like enormous needles crossing the sky, make the towers the most characteristic element of the temple, with its shape cutting through the city sky-line. For this reason, the temple of the Sagrada Familia exceeds in majesty any other Christian church which has been built up to now.

Judas, sculpture on the apostle's bell tower

The temple towers

Their enormous spires define Barcelona's panorama

The exterior of the monument holds an extraordinary symbolism which Gaudí knew how to give expression to with four models of towers. The four rising from the three façades represent the twelve apostles. Over the temple is situated the highest tower which symbolizes Jesus. This is surrounded by four cimborios which are dedicated to the evangelists. Lastly, the apse is covered by a large tower dedicated to Mary.

View from the mountain. Owing to their great height, the towers of Sagrada Familia dominate the urban landscape.

The lighthouse of Barcelona

Gaudí wanted Sagrada Familia to be higher than any other civil building in the city to show the supremacy of the divine over the human. The temple had to be the urban landscape's reference point, and be visible from any point in Barcelona. To achieve this, the central cimborio was planned, dedicated to Jesus, measuring 170 metres high, just a few metres less than the mountain Montjuïc, as according to the architect: man can't outdo what God has created.

1925

THE FIRST BELL TOWER IS FINISHED

The Saint Barnabus tower was the first to be built and the only one that Gaudí saw completed.

The temple monument in 1910

Illustration of the temple exterior by Joan Rubió, one of the architects who assisted Gaudí.

 COMPARISON
THE TEMPLE AND OTHER STRUCTURES

The central tower of Sagrada Familia, dedicated to Jesus, soars higher than many of the most emblematic monuments in the world.

 Pisa Tower **55 m**

 Statue of Liberty **93 m**

 Big Ben **98 m**

 Sagrada Familia **170 m**

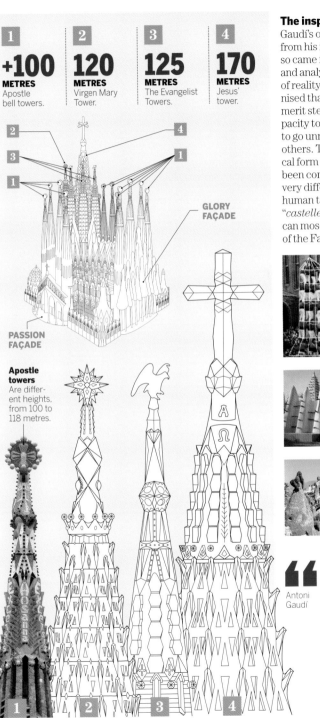

1	**2**	**3**	**4**
+100 METRES Apostle bell towers.	**120** METRES Virgen Mary Tower.	**125** METRES The Evangelist Towers.	**170** METRES Jesus' tower.

GLORY
FAÇADE

PASSION
FAÇADE

Apostle towers
Are different heights, from 100 to 118 metres.

The inspiration

Gaudí's originality surged from his imagination, but also came from his penetrating and analytical observation of reality. He himself recognised that a great part of his merit stemmed from his capacity to observe what tends to go unnoticed by many others. The singular conical form of the towers has been compared with three very different realities: the human towers made by the "*castellers*", the north African mosques and the Valley of the Fairies, in Turkey.

The castellers
Gaudí confirmed that his towers obeyed the same law of equilibrium as the human towers or "*castells*", a deep rooted tradition in Catalonia.

The Africa Mosque
In 1892, Gaudí travelled to Tangiers where he came across this type of construction.

The Valley of the Fairies, Turkey
Gaudí was also inspired by these curious geological formations.

> The shape of the towers, vertical and parabolic, is the union of gravity with light... in the upper part there will be luminous lights, like the natural light which comes from the sky"
>
> Antoni Gaudí

The bell towers

Are located on the Nativity, Passion and Glory façade and represent Jesus' twelve apostles.

The bell tower terminations

Gaudí thought of two complex solutions for the twelve bell tower endings. The first one consisted of a look-out tower with a hexagonal base and pyramidal shape with rings. The second proposal, which was the one chosen in the end and carried out, meant that each tower was topped with a pinnacle decorated with Venetian polychromatic mosaic work and crowned with a double-sided shield, a cross and white spheres, in reference to the Episcopal mitre.

The shield
The termination of the pinnacle is a double-sided shield with a golden cross and on one of the sides is the apostle's initial who the tower is dedicated to.

The hollow for the floodlights
This area is designed to hold two lights: one beaming towards the street and the other towards the central cimborios to illuminate them at night.

Prayers
On each ending there are six vertical signs which alternately read *Hosanna* and *Excelsis*. Each letter is written in a hexagonal square.

Pinnacle

Vents to direct the sound
Gaudí tilted the ledges of the windows in order that the sound of the bells would be heard throughout the city.

The apostle Barnabus
Each bell tower carries the name and apostle that it represents.

The Passion apostles
The sculptures of the apostles on the bell towers on the Passion façade are by Josep Maria Subirachs.

James the Lesser

Bartholomew

Thomas

Philip

LOCATION

The mitre
The mitre or head-dress worn by bishops is represented by the double-sided cross decorated with white balls.

The pinnacles
Measuring 25 metres high, the tower pinnacles stand out from the rest of the bell towers for the complex shapes they adopt and the rich-coloured mosaic patterns they are covered with. Gaudí used them to unite the symbols which represent bishops: cross, mitre, staff and ring. Bishops are represented in the bell towers because they are responsible for carrying on the work of the first apostles.

The staff
The higher trunk of the pinnacle leans a little in its upper part to simulate the curved shape of the staff.

The phrases
Over the bell towers, the word *Sanctus* is repeated. Each group of three *Sanctus* is dedicated to the Father, the Son and the Holy Spirit.

DATA
THE PINNACLE GLASS

The ring
A symbol of authority, the Episcopal ring is below the pinnacle trunk.

The Venetian glass
To decorate the pinnacles, Gaudí chose Venetian mosaic , which is characterized for the fine quality glass which it is made from. It comes from Murano, an island world famous for its strong elegant glass, handcrafted since the 15th century.

Inside the bell towers

Propelled by his non-conformist spirit, Gaudí carried out an acoustic study so that the sound from the bells would be perfect.

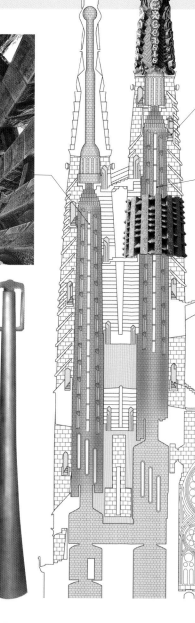

Cross section of the bell towers

The temple's voice

Gaudí wanted the bell towers to be the voice of the temple, which meant they had to have a finely tuned sound and be heard throughout the city. He therefore experimented with different types. He finally decided that the temple would have three varieties of bells: common ones, some tuned to the notes *mi*, *sol* and *do* and tubular ones.

The tubular bell

The tubular bells will be fixed and struck by hammers triggered by an electronic mechanism connected to a keyboard, as if it were an enormous piano which, moreover, will be able to reproduce any note.

The walkways

The bell towers on this façade are connected by means of bridges and raised walkways.

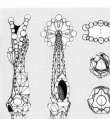

> **This mosaic explosion is the first thing that sailors will see on approaching Barcelona, It will be a radiant welcome!"**
>
> Antoni Gaudí

The interior
The stairs climb between the outer walls of the tower. The hollow inside is reserved for the bell.

Space for the bells
The temple will have 60 bells which will hang inside the bell towers, where they will obtain their optimum acoustic rendition.

The base
The bell towers of the Nativity façade have a square base, but after 20 metres (approximately a fifth of their height), they become a circular shape.

Interior corridor
At a certain height in the bell towers, there is a corridor which the stairs pass through.

WHAT IS A PINNACLE?
The pinnacles are columns finished in pyramidal form which are used to crown some of the towers.

The winding staircase

The winding snail-shape stairs are situated in the lower part of the bell towers. Due to their narrowness, one has the sensation of going back on oneself. In order to create a much more interesting effect, Antoni Gaudí planned that in each pair of bell towers the stairs would turn in opposite directions. The winding staircases reach the height of the balconies and from then on, the stairs cling to the exterior walls, given that the hollow in the centre of the tower is reserved for the bells.

Nature
Gaudí managed to reproduce nature with a surprising accuracy, as can be observed when you compare the photo above (section of a snail shell) with the stairs.

426
STEPS
are in the towers. Climbing them requires a great physical effort but is more than compensated for by their magnificent views.

HISTORIC
CONSTRUCTION OF THE BELL TOWERS

The first bell towers to be built were those of the Nativity façade. The only tower that Gaudí saw completed out of the four towers, was the tower dedicated to Saint Barnabus which was finished in 1925, a year before he died. Work on the towers of the Passion façade was finished in 1978.

The cimborios

The group of six central cimborios are the means by which the temple exterior reaches its maximum expression.

Jesus' tower

The central cimborio represents Jesus and thus is the most monumental of all. From its top part the words *Amén* and *Aleluya* will descend, and as a symbol of the triumph of Christ it will be topped off by an enormous 4 armed cross which will reach 15 metres high. In its central part the cross will contain a lamb. The striking Venetian mosaics on its roof will make the cimborio gleam in the sunlight.

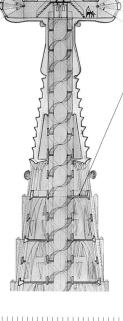

Night time illumination
From the four arms of the cross will shine four powerful beams of light which will be visible far away.

Floors
The central cimborio is divided horizontally into thirteen floors.

Quintana the architect
Assistant to Gaudí, he did a study drawing of the tower on a four metre long sheet of paper, which meant he had to do it on the floor.

 PROCESS
CONSTRUCTION OF THE CIMBORIOS

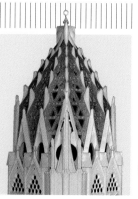

The sacristy as an experiment for the cimborios
The six central towers have a structure which is similar to the sacristies, although on a larger scale. For this reason, Gaudí had foreseen that the construction of the sacristy would act as an experiment to define the shape and the details of the cimborios. This way, they could also study the possible problems that could come about when more height was added.

The four armed cross
The three-dimensional cross developed by Gaudí was repeatedly used in many of his works.

Bellesguard

Park Güell

Casa Batlló

LOCATION

Saint John tower
Symbolized by an eagle.

Saint Mark tower
Symbolized by a lion.

Saint Matthew tower
Symbolized by an angel.

Saint Luke tower
Symbolized by an ox.

The Evangelist towers

The cimborios dedicated to the evangelists surround Jesus, reminding us that they were the ones who were chosen to spread the word of Jesus. Each cimborio will be crowned by the symbol which best represents its evangelist. At night, two spotlights will come from these towers: one will illuminate the street (symbolic of the light from the Gospel illuminating men) and another towards the tower of Jesus, to remind the world of his divinity.

?

WHAT IS A CIMBORIO?
Cimborios are towers with a squared or octagonal base which are raised above the cross section of a church or temple with the objective of illuminating its interior.

Mary's tower

The cimborio which is dedicated to the Virgin Mary will be on the apse side, following Byzantine tradition. The most spectacular element of this tower will be the star crowning it.
It will be a large shining star which will represent the *Stella matutina* (the morning star), symbolizing that, just like this star announces dawn, Mary preceded the coming of Jesus.

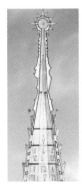
Cross section
The interior of the cimborio of Mary.

> The inscriptions will be like an entwining tape which will climb up the towers. All those that read them, including the sceptics, will sing a hymn to the Holy Trinity"

Antoni Gaudí

The decoration
The pinnacle of Mary's tower is covered with a polychromatic mosaic of blues, reds and gold.

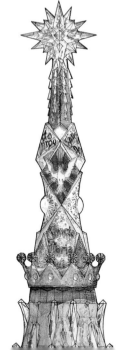

THE SIGNIFICANCE OF THE TEMPLE TOWERS

The pillars of the Catholic faith are represented by the temple towers: Jesus, Mary, the four writers of the New Testament and the apostles.

The Evangelists

The Evangelists were responsible for the narration of Jesus' life. The union of the four accounts form part of the New Testament.

1 Jesus

Is the Son of God and the founder of Christianity, symbolized by Gaudí with the highest tower crowned with the cross.

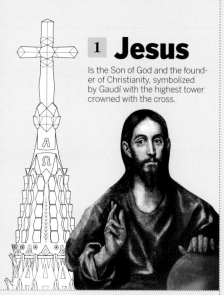

MATTHEW
Was apostle to Jesus Christ and the author of the first Gospel. His traditional symbol is an angel.

3

MARK
Is the author of the second Gospel and is symbolized by a lion. He was Saint Peter's interpreter.

4

2 Mary

The virginity of the mother of Jesus is one of the main Catholic dogmas. It is represented by the apse tower which is crowned with a bright star.

LUKE
Author of the third Gospel and symbolized by an ox. He was companion to Saint Peter.

5

JOHN
Symbolized by the eagle, he was apostle to Jesus. He is the author of the fourth Gospel and the Apocalypse.

6

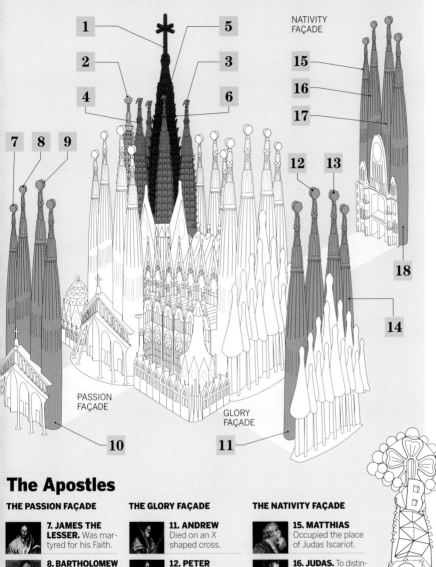

NATIVITY
FAÇADE

1

5

2

3

4

6

15

16

17

7 8 9

12 13

18

14

PASSION
FAÇADE

GLORY
FAÇADE

10

11

The Apostles

THE PASSION FAÇADE

7. JAMES THE LESSER. Was martyred for his Faith.

8. BARTHOLOMEW Went to preach in India and Arabia.

9. THOMAS Doubted Christ's resurrection.

10. PHILIP One of the first disciples.

THE GLORY FAÇADE

11. ANDREW Died on an X shaped cross.

12. PETER Was chosen to create the Church.

13. PAUL Was the first Christian theologian.

14. JAMES THE GREATER John's brother.

THE NATIVITY FAÇADE

15. MATTHIAS Occupied the place of Judas Iscariot.

16. JUDAS. To distinguish him he is called Judas Thaddaeus.

17. SIMON His symbol is a saw.

18. BARNABUS Preached in Asia Minor and Cyprus.

01

01. Pinnacle of the apostle Matthias. Complex forms decorated with Venetian glass, the pinnacles represent bishops, for it is they who continue the mission of the apostles. **02. The word *Sanctus*.** Situated on the bell towers, each group of three *Sanctus* is dedicated to the Father, the Son and the Holy Spirit. **03. The vents.** The towers are completed covered by sound vents which direct the chimes of the bells all over the city. **04. Star-like pinnacle.** This pinnacle which is above the sculpture of the apostle Simon tops off the niches. **05. Inside the bell tower.** The bell towers are designed to hold tubular bells which can reproduce any musical note.

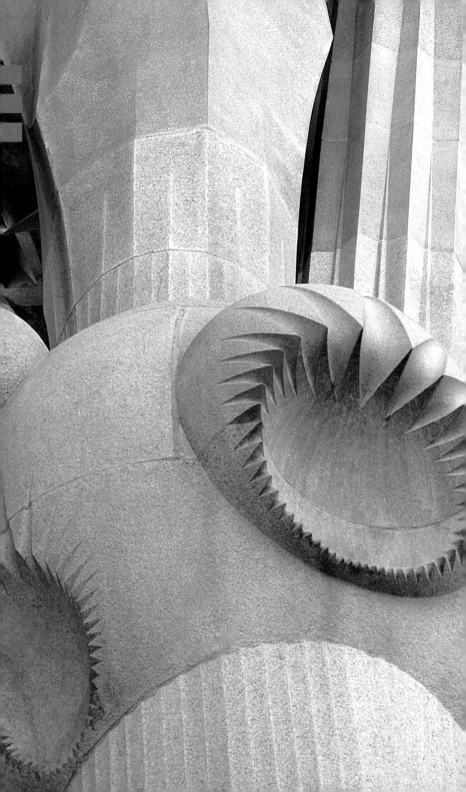

09

THE TEMPLE INTERIOR

A harmonious and innovative temple

The essence of Gaudí's architecture is concentrated inside the Sagrada Familia.

The Latin cross ground plan is the only concession that Gaudí made to classical structures inside the temple. The rest of the architectonic elements which make it up are, as the majority of Gaudí's work, totally original.

The first project for the temple naves, which was presented in 1898, was basically Gothic style, although the need for buttresses had been corrected. Due to an in-depth study of weights, Gaudí managed to transfer the pressure of the vaults directly towards the floor by means of extremely canted arches. Nevertheless, this project didn't fully satisfy the architect for two reasons: the temple continued being, in essence, gothically influenced and each arch mechanically depended on the adjoining one, so if one failed, it would drag the others down in its fall. At the age of 70, Gaudí found the solution

that he so yearned for in arborescent columns. These columns, tilted and branched like a tree, allowed the avoidance of buttresses while at the same time the weight of the roof was directed to the floor, liberating the outer walls. This ingenious architectural system has, likewise, a spectacular aesthetic consequence, as the temple interior is transformed into an enormous stone forest, where light harmoniously filters through the vaults and exterior walls.

A knot carved in stone

The temple interior

Gaudí conceived it as a colossal mystic forest

Just like on the temple exterior, Gaudí bestowed a symbolic value on each element inside the temple. The whole monument is an exaltation of the Faith and represents the universal Church. With its tree-like columns, Gaudí wanted the Sagrada Familia to be an enormous spiritual forest, a place of prayer, where the believer feels protected and united with God.

The symbolic dimension

Inside the temple the four daily prayers will be represented, just like the Gospels and epistles which are read out in Sunday mass. The Holy Spirit will be symbolized by a large lamp which will illuminate the altar, presided over by a cross. A branch will come out sustaining the altar, and the Calvary of Jesus will be above it. The apse cupola will be covered by a mosaic symbolizing the vestments of God on its celestial vault.

Arborescent columns
Each column will carry the image of a saint which will appear to move upwards to heaven. From the upper part, the angels will descend towards earth.

The interior
This illustration by Berenguer shows the altar area. This altar will be below a triumphant arch from which will hang a baldachin.

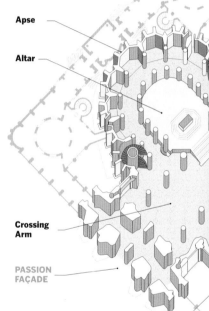

Apse

Altar

Crossing Arm

PASSION FAÇADE

4.500
SQUARE METRES
surface area, will hold around 14,000 visitors in the temple interior.

Nave lateral façade

Original model by Gaudí
The current construction work on the temple is based on models Gaudí made when carrying out his investigations.

1 The fruit on the exterior
The vertexes of the walls are crowned by baskets containing different fruits, such as lemons, figs, apples and cherries. These elements symbolize the fruit that the Holy Spirit scattered on the earth.

Choir

NATIVITY FAÇADE

Nave lateral façade

Aisle

Nave

Aisle

GLORY FAÇADE

The Nativity lateral façade
In the interior part there will be choir galleries.

Phrases on the exterior
Between the windows words are written such as *oració* (prayer), *thus* (incense) and *aurum* (gold).

The lateral façades of the naves

Thanks to the ingenious system of construction that Gaudí applied in the interior, the side walls are liberated from supporting the weight of the temple roofs. This way, they only have to support their own structure, which means they can be lighter. All the walls are dotted with numerous windows of diverse sizes which harmoniously illuminate the temple naves.

The founding saints
On the exterior, on the upper part between the windows are the statues of founding saints of religious orders. There are ten in total.

Saint Juan Bosco

Saint Joaquina of Vedruna

Saint José Oriol

The five naves

Gaudí highlighted the temple's symbolic and spiritual importance by endowing it with spectacular dimensions.

A temple of huge dimensions

The temple has a Latin cross ground plan and is made up of five naves, with a crossing measuring 60 metres long and 45 metres wide. The total length of the temple, from the entrance to the apse, is 90 metres long. The central nave vaults measure 45 metres high, while the central cimborio vaults reach 60 metres. With these dimensions, the Sagrada Familia will be one of the largest temples in the world.

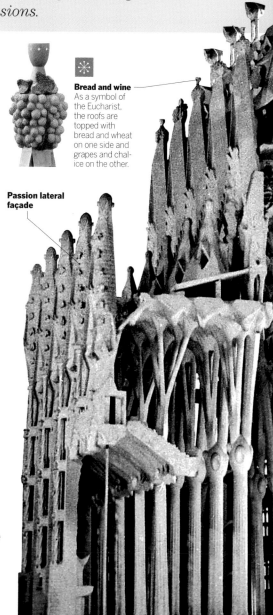

Bread and wine
As a symbol of the Eucharist, the roofs are topped with bread and wheat on one side and grapes and chalice on the other.

Passion lateral façade

The windows
Some windows recall the rose windows of Gothic cathedrals.

" The temple interior will be like a forest"

Antoni Gaudí

Location
The main entrance to the temple is on the Glory façade, whose five doors correspond with the five naves.

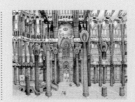

Drawing of the interior
This illustration by Berenguer shows the doorway of the Nativity façade. On the left the altar can be seen.

1.200

PEOPLE SINGING
make up the adult chorus. The child choir will be made up of 350 children.

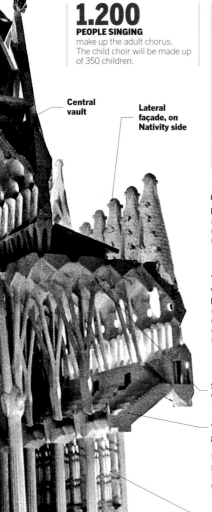

Central vault

Lateral façade, on Nativity side

Side vault

The Choir gallery
The stands have the necessary gradient so that the altar can be easily seen.

Window
To illuminate the temple, Gaudí included numerous windows.

?

WHAT IS A NAVE?
The naves are spaces between two rows of arches. The central nave is the one in the centre of the temple going from the main entrance up to the apse.

45

METRES
is the height of the central nave.

30

METRES
is the height of the vaults of the four lateral naves.

The Choir

Located on the lateral naves is the gallery for the adult choir, who will sing in big celebrations. The choir gallery is focused towards the large altar and is accessed by means of a winding staircase. The child choir will be located on the apse side and be comprised of 350 children.

 CHRONOLOGY
CONSTRUCTION PROGRESS

1987
Work starts on the nave foundations.

1989
Various pillars and lateral windows are erected.

1997
On completion of the lateral vaults, work on the central one commences.

The columns

With the arborescent column, Gaudí succeeded in discovering the mechanical solution and aesthetic spirit he desired for his temple.

Arborescent column

The new column

Gaudí investigated for many years until he discovered a column which would mean he could avoid the use of buttresses. One of these innovations consisted in slightly tilting the columns in order to capture the weight of the roof in the most optimum way. Likewise, he turned the shaft in two directions to achieve a better resistance and a spectacular aesthetic effect.

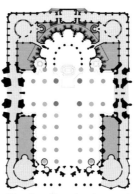

Plan view of temple columns

DATA
TYPES OF TEMPLE COLUMN

In relation to the weight that they had to sustain. Gaudí gave a different base and type of stone to each column.

	6 sided base	8 sided base	10 sided base	12 sided base
	6	8	10	12
Diameter	1,05 m	1,40 m	1,75 m	2,10 m
Support	200 ton.	1.000 ton.	3.000 ton.	6.000 ton.
Type of stone	Montjuic	Granite	Basalt	Porfid
Colour	Light grey	Blueish grey	Dark grey	Reddish
The photo				

A first study
Gaudí experimented with tilting and helicoid columns in Park Güell and various other works.

The reference
Gaudí wanted the interior of the temple to possess the beauty and intimacy of a lush forest.

36
COLUMNS
support the temple vaults. The largest are the four which are on the cross-section of the temple.

22,20
METRES
is the height of the tallest columns. The smallest measure half the size: 11.10 metres.

The arborescent column
As Gaudí wanted his columns to possess the robustness and beauty of trees, he fled from vertical rigidity by tilting and turning them in spiral form, the same way that tree trunks grow. Likewise, when they reached a certain height, the columns branched out in a very precise manner to support the vaults covering the temple naves.

Nature as master
Gaudí achieved great architectonic solutions by emulating nature.

?
WHAT IS A NODE?
The nodes or knots are the elements of transition between columns. Gaudí used them to mark the point where the columns branch out.

COMPARISON
NEW COLUMN CREATED BY GAUDÍ

The styles
The column has experienced an evolution throughout the history of architecture. Gaudí dedicated many years of investigation to the creation of a new column which would exceed any previous order, not only in its capacity to support weight, but also in its beauty.

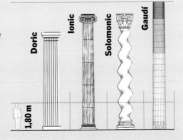

Doric
Ionic
Solomonic
Gaudí

1,80 m

The vaults

As perfect culmination of the arborescent structure, Gaudí transformed the temple vaults into palm leaves.

Lengthy research
Gaudí spent a lot of time and effort finding the perfect solution for the vaults.

The vaults

In contrast to former cathedrals, whose vaults were robust and had to support a lot of weight, Gaudí wanted Sagrada Familia's vaults to be light-weight and illuminate the temple interior. The vaults emerge from tree-like columns and form palm leaves which represent the symbol of martyrdom. The assembly point of the leaves, some concave and others convex, also allow the filtering of light into the temple.

Azimuthal view of the vaults
The star-like vaults have orifices through which light enters.

1924
THE DEFINITIVE SOLUTION
Gaudí abandoned the idea of the ribbed vault system for the hyperbolic vault system.

Study model. Original by Gaudí (1920-1926).

PROCESS
MODULATION OF THE VAULTS

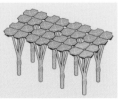

The vaults are formed by module repetition. This system facilitated construction and lightened structure, as by being independent, each vault only supports its own weight.

Original model by Antoni Gaudí
As in the rest of the temple, Gaudí used models to carry out the study on the vaults.

Computer simulation
In the current construction work the original models are combined with the latest technology.

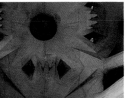

Central nave roofs
A study of the roof and windows, original model by Gaudí.

The roofs

The central nave's ceiling is comprised of a series of pyramids, each one crowned with a lantern and light, reaching 70 metres high. Built with Montjuïc stone, they will be decorated with shields, similar to those on the bell towers and have the inscription *Amen* and *Al-le-lu-ia*.

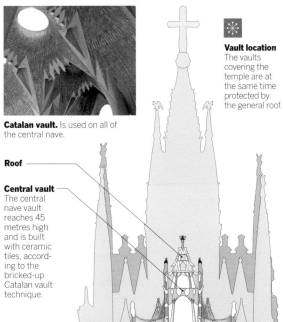

Catalan vault. Is used on all of the central nave.

Vault location
The vaults covering the temple are at the same time protected by the general roof.

Roof

Central vault
The central nave vault reaches 45 metres high and is built with ceramic tiles, according to the bricked-up Catalan vault technique.

Lateral vaults
The lateral vaults are 30 metres high and are made of concrete.

The illumination

Gaudí used light to achieve artistic effects and accentuate the temple's mysticism.

The temple of light

The windows, the vaults and, in general, all the sources of light were designed to illuminate the temple interior the same way as light filters through the leaves in a forest. Gaudí pursued a harmonious indirect illumination, which highlighted the plasticity of the architecture, while at the same time showed off the temple's decoration and transmitted a feeling of spiritual peace.

Natural light
Sun light will illuminate the temple in a gentle and harmonious manner thanks to the curious shape and arrangement of the vaults, which act like luminance diffusers, and by the windows which go round the temple.

The evolution of the windows

In consonance with their creator's artistic search, the windows experience a clear evolution from the neo-gothic style of the crypt to the reinterpretation of the Gothic that Gaudí made in those of the central nave.

Gothic
In the lower windows, although possessing new shapes, the Gothic structure is retained, with its honeycomb shape and large circular rose window.

Electrical illumination
The lights are positioned and designed to illuminate as natural light does.

 The light in temples only has to be the necessary, given that in a temple there must be withdrawal, and very bright lights distract and create restlessness"

Antoni Gaudí

LIGHT DIFFUSERS
Fitted into the holes of the vault are light diffusers invented by Gaudí. They are a type of lamp made from metal mesh which are used to diffuse sun light in the interior and illuminate the surface of the vaults. Their other function is to artificially light the temple at night.

Light diffusers
They are decorated with Jesus, Joseph and Marys' anagrams.

Stained Glass
With beautiful colours and marked shapes, they are the work of Catalan artist Joan Vila-Grau.

2
Geometric
The evolution towards a honeycomb shape gives way to new geometric forms, with a triangular fronton topping the window.

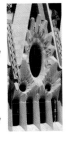

3
Geometric naturalism
The last window clearly shows the leap towards abstraction, in such a way that the number of elements is greatly simplified.

CHRONOLOGICAL EVOLUTION OF WORK ON THE TEMPLE

More than a century old, the Sagrada Familia has witnessed all types of historical events, while its construction advances on.

1940, restoration of the models

The first stone
On Saint Joseph day, work starts on the temple.

The Rosary Portal
Its decoration is concluded.

The Nativity bell towers
Reach 82 metres high. In 1930 they will be completed.

1882 1891 1897 1899 1915 1920 1940

Work starts on apse
After the crypt, work commences on the apse.

Nativity façade
They start adding the sculptures. The first are the angels and trumpeters.

Letters on the towers
The first letter is put into place on the bell tower dedicated to Saint Barnabus.

1903
The Massacre of the Innocents
The plaster model is put into position and after its study is later produced in stone.

1933
The Tree of Life
The cypress tree and lantern of Faith are finished on the Nativity façade.

1973
The Passion bell towers. Reach 57 metres. The rose windows are added with Venetian mosaic.

2004
The temple grows
24 windows, 225 columns and 130 nave skylights have already been erected.

Lateral vaults
The lateral naves are covered by the vaults.

| 1954 | 1973 | 1958 | 1986 | 1995 | 1999 | 2005 | 2...... |

Passion façade
Construction commences on the Passion façade based on Gaudí's drawings and explanations.

Construction on the naves
Work is started on the column foundations.

Central vault
The highest vaults on the main nave are built.

New cloisters
Construction work advances on the cloister.

1958
Sculpture of the nativity
On Saint Joseph's day the sculptural group by Joan Busquets is put into position.

1978
Nave windows
They begin to raise the exterior windows.

1990
Subirach's sculptures
The sculptures are put into place on the Passion façade.

01. Nodes and vaults. Like a tree, the column supports a foliage of vaults. **02. Walls and windows.** A gallery goes around the interior walls of the temple. **03 and 04. The stones.** Gaudí positioned blocks of stone of basic shape to be sculpted later on. **05. Nativity stained glass.** From outside you can make out the colours of the windows, work by Joan Vila-Grau. **06. Light diffuser.** The holes in the vaults hold diffusers invented by Gaudí. **07. Stained glass.** Glass panes from the main window of the Passion façade, by Joan Vila-Grau. **08. Tears.** Located in the inside part of the Nativity façade. **09. Catalan vault.** These are the central nave vaults and are built with ceramic tiles.

10

The schoolrooms

One of the most simple and ingenious buildings by Gaudí

In a corner of the grounds of Sagrada Familia there is a building of apparent modesty and small dimensions. *Las Escuelas* (the schoolrooms), which Gaudí designed, were built for the children of the workmen and families of the neighbourhood. The simplicity of this construction is deceptive, given that, as with all of Gaudí's work, its exterior reflects the aesthetic originality of its creator and its structure, his innovative technical solutions.

Simple and rational

The schoolrooms were built between 1908 and 1909 and functioned as a teaching centre for more than 70 years. Their external appearance is of great simplicity as their demolishment was foreseen as soon as more space was needed in the temple grounds and Gaudí also wanted minimal cost. The most distinctive feature of the building is its undulating roof and walls. The sinuous form provides the structure with a great resistance in a simple and rational way. For example, the walls offer an appearance of great rigidity, in spite of being built with two layers of vertically positioned brick.

The roof
The roof's undulations allow the water to pour out on either side in an original and practical way.

Entrance
View of a door which provides access to the construction's interior.

1936
THE SCHOOL-ROOMS
catch fire along with other parts of the Sagrada Familia, at the start of the Civil War.

> **The Mediterraneans are the only ones who have understood geometry..."**

Antoni Gaudí

Drawings generated by computer
The school's roof and wall undulations, where the uneven height of the walls can be seen.

Materials and dimensions
Built with brick, one of Gaudí's preferred materials. Its maximum height reaches six metres and its base occupies a space of 24 x 12 metres.

9.000
PESETAS
was how much it cost to build the schoolrooms. It is believed that Gaudí paid the 9000 pesetas from his own pocket (around 54 euros.)

2002
IN THIS YEAR
The schoolrooms are moved some metres to make space for the construction work on the Sagrada Familia temple. In the process, they are made to look like how they were originally.

Past and present
At the start of the Spanish Civil War, the schoolrooms are affected by a fire which leads to grave consequences for Gaudí's work. Their original appearance is finally recuperated when they are moved in 2002. Since then, they have held the exhibition where some of Gaudí's contributions to architecture can be seen.

HISTORIC
STUDIES BY LE CORBUSIER IN 1928

Considered as the father of modern architecture, the Swiss architect Le Corbusier marvelled at Gaudí's schoolrooms when he visited the temple in 1928.

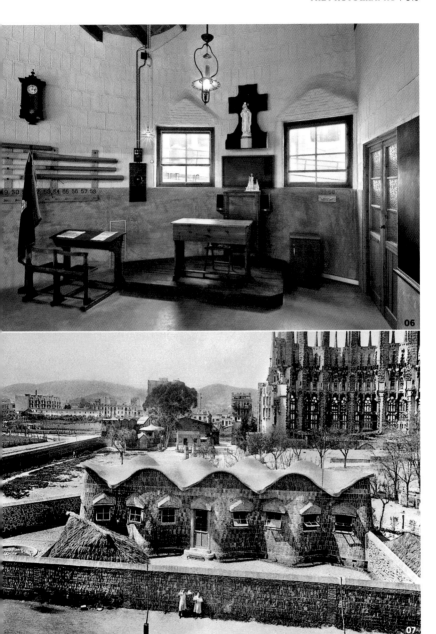

06

07

01. Windows. Gaudí planned the school as a simple and economic construction, as demonstrated by its windows: it would be demolished when construction work advanced. **02. Undulating roof.** The sinuous shape fortifies the construction in a simple and rational way. **03. Accessory.** A fake bell is next to one of the entrance doors. **04. Rainfall drainage.** The endings of the undulating roof also function as a means of draining away rain water. **05. Lamp.** A room still retains period lamps. **06. The class.** The interior has three schoolrooms, which can hold up to 150 pupils. **07. Historic photo.** The schools before the fire in 1936.

VISUAL GUIDE TO THE
TEMPLE OF LA SAGRADA FAMILIA

© PUBLISHED BY
2006, MUNDO FLIP EDICIONES, S.C.P.

TEXTS
MANAGING DIRECTORS:
CARLOS GIORDANO AND NICOLÁS PALMISANO
REDACTION: MARÍA JOSÉ GÓMEZ GIMENO
TRANSLATIONS: CERYS R. JONES
© CARLOS GIORDANO AND NICOLÁS PALMISANO

PHOTOGRAPHS
CARLOS GIORDANO AND NICOLÁS PALMISANO

© PHOTOGRAPHS OF TEMPLE INTERIOR AND MUSEUM
CARLOS GIORDANO, NICOLÁS PALMISANO AND JUNTA
CONSTRUCTORA DEL TEMPLE EXPIATORI DE LA SAGRADA FAMÍLIA

© ARCHIVE PHOTOGRAPHS
JUNTA CONSTRUCTORA DEL TEMPLE EXPIATORI
DE LA SAGRADA FAMÍLIA

© ILLUSTRATIONS AND PLANS
CARLOS GIORDANO AND NICOLÁS PALMISANO
(PAG. 22, 24, 25, 26, 34, 36, 46, 49, 50, 53, 54, 62, 76, 77,
86, 100, 109, 110, 111, 112, 115, 117, 124, 128, 130 Y 140).

© ARCHITECTONIC WORK
JUNTA CONSTRUCTORA DEL TEMPLE DE LA
SAGRADA FAMÍLIA AND ARXIU DEL TEMPLE

ACKNOWLEDGMENTS
JUNTA CONSTRUCTORA DEL TEMPLE DE LA
SAGRADA FAMÍLIA AND ARXIU DEL TEMPLE

THIRD EDITION, 2006

ISBN
84-933983-5-7

DEPÓSITO LEGAL
B-27365-2005

PRINTED IN SPAIN
I.G. MARMOL S.L.

Temple Expiatori de la
SAGRADA FAMÍLIA

WITH THE
COLLABORATION OF THE
JUNTA CONSTRUCTORA
DEL TEMPLE EXPIATORI
DE LA SAGRADA FAMILIA

**MUNDO FLIP
EDICIONES**
www.mundoflip.com
info@mundoflip.com